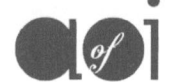

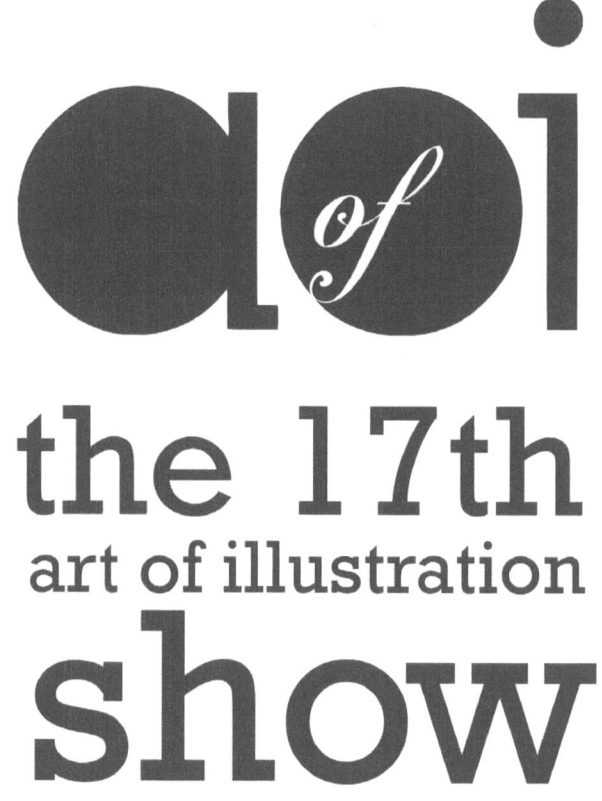

the 17th
art of illustration
show

Table of Contents

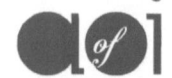

INTRODUCTION

As illustrators, we come equipped with an innate desire to tell stories. This desire manifests itself in our drive, in our professionalism, and in our deliverance. At CCAD we produce work that not only are we proud of, but work that we can't help sharing with each other and with you.

This year the Art of Illustration show, commonly referred to as "AOI", continued to grow. The submission numbers were bigger and the diversity of pieces amplified to fresh and exciting heights. AOI was started seventeen years ago in 1997 by students for students and has been a staple event for CCAD's Illustration department ever since.

We received over three hundred submissions this year ranging in style, technique, and branching across all of the majors. As in previous years, after collecting all of the pieces, a select group of accredited judges score and determine the winners. Then, with the assistance of the student committee the show is organized, arranged, and brought to fruition. The show has been held at Rivet Gallery in Columbus' Short North for several years now and has helped AOI grow in attendance and notability. Along with a reception for family and friends, selected prizes are given to students for first, second, and third place. Judges also select their favorites among the winners to deem their "judges pick".

With pieces this year that span the illustrative spectrum, CCAD boasts a selection that proves an inherent desire to produce and be surrounded by quality storytelling. We can only hope that the show continues to grow in diversity and number and that AOI will remain a celebrated CCAD tradition for many years to come.

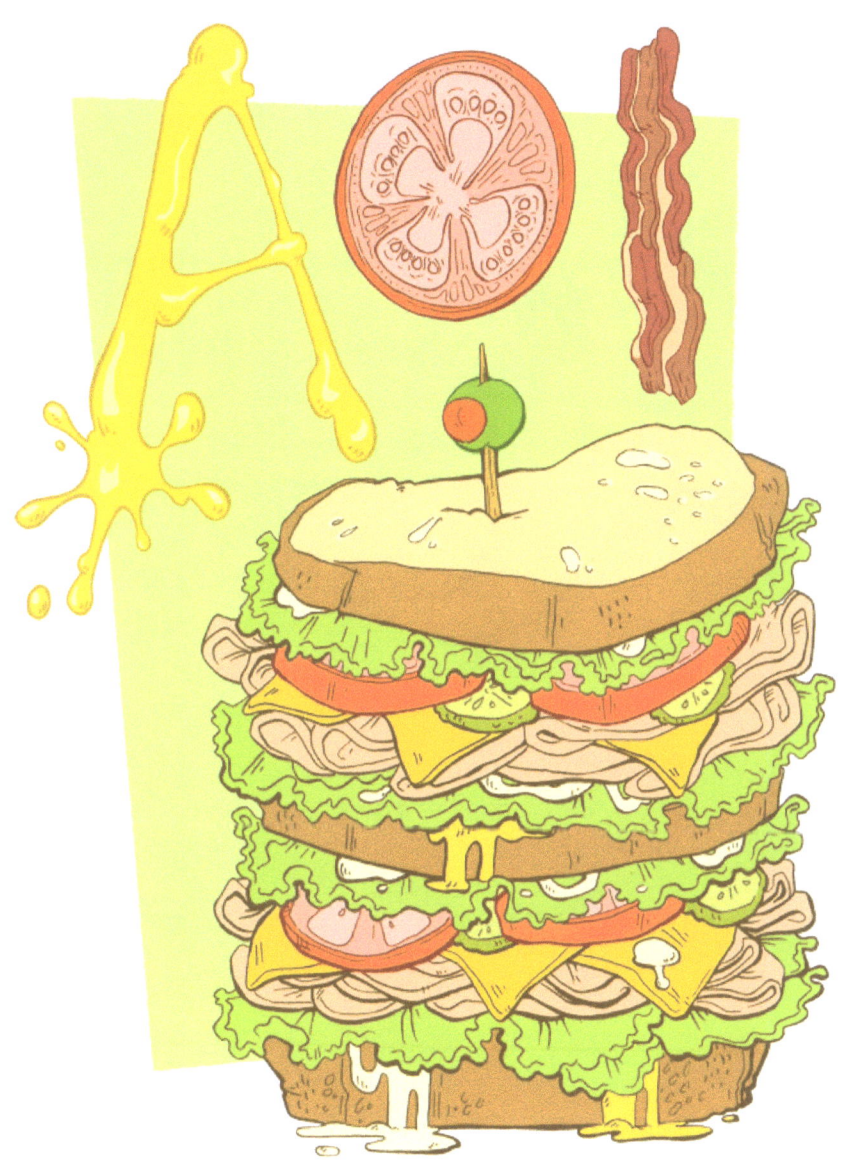

Poster Design
Hollyanne Shell

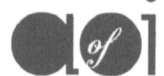

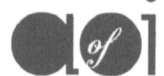

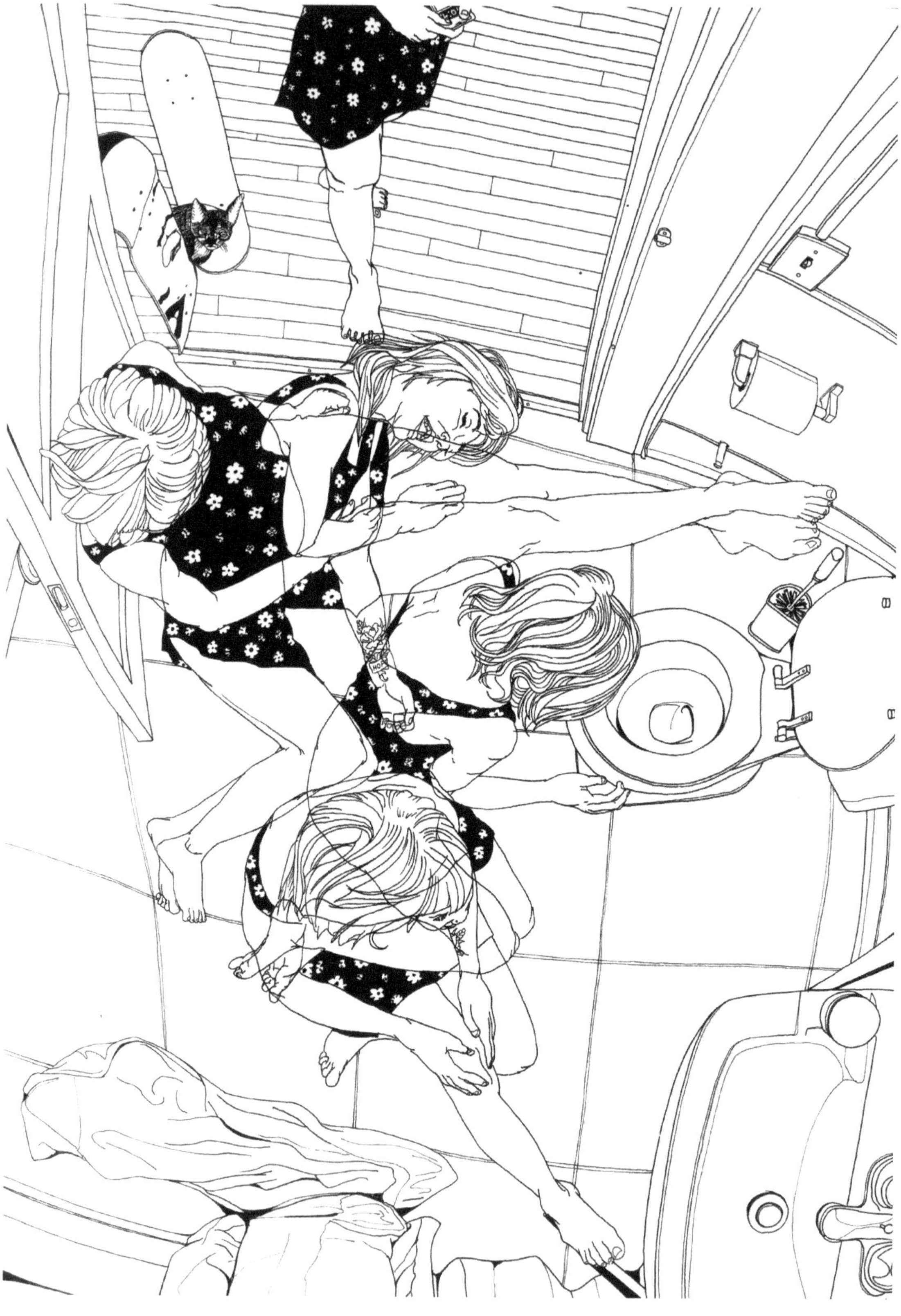

Hope
Aaron Behnk

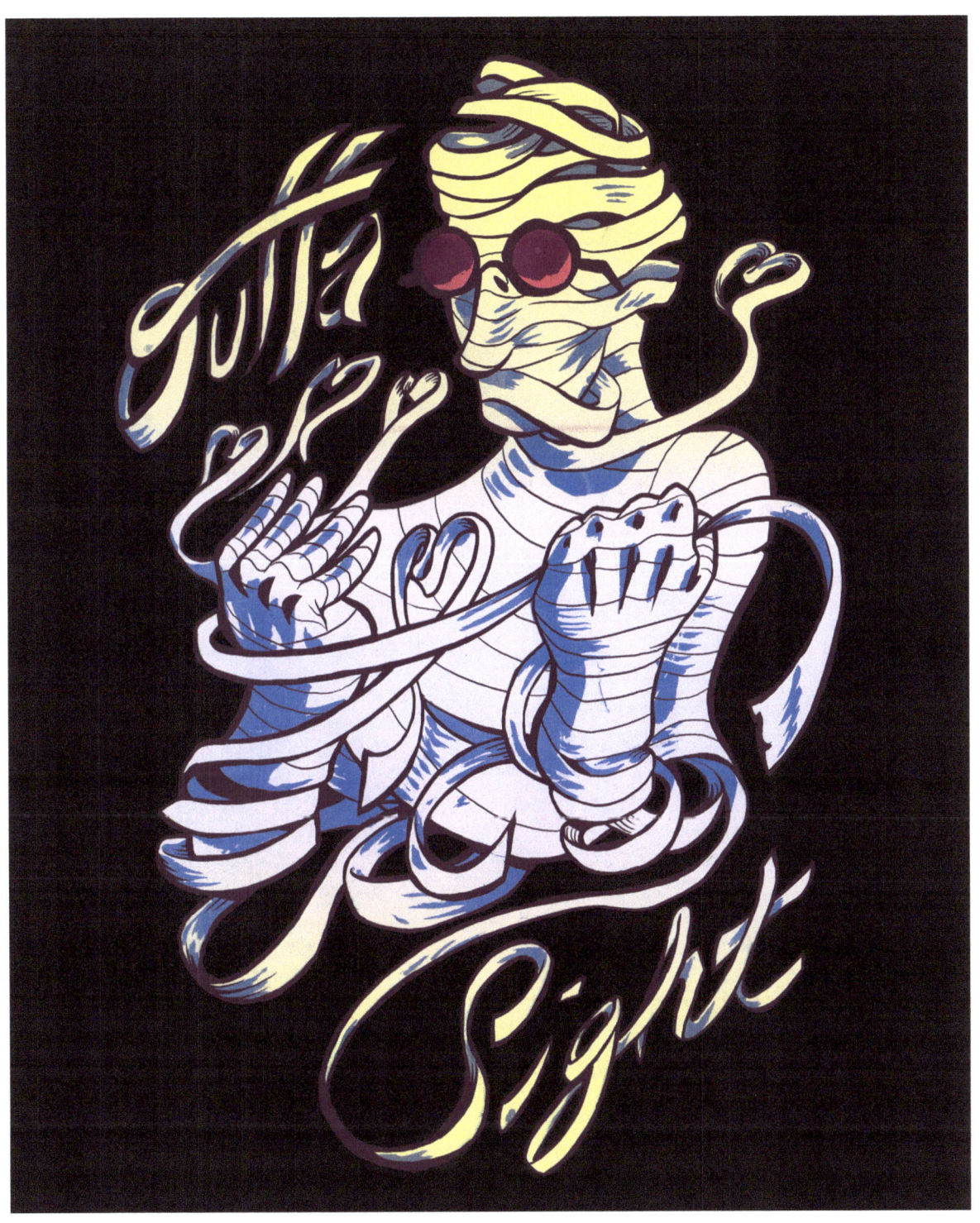

The Romantic Mr. Griffin
Dorian Lafferre

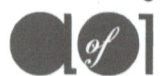

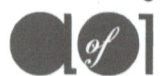

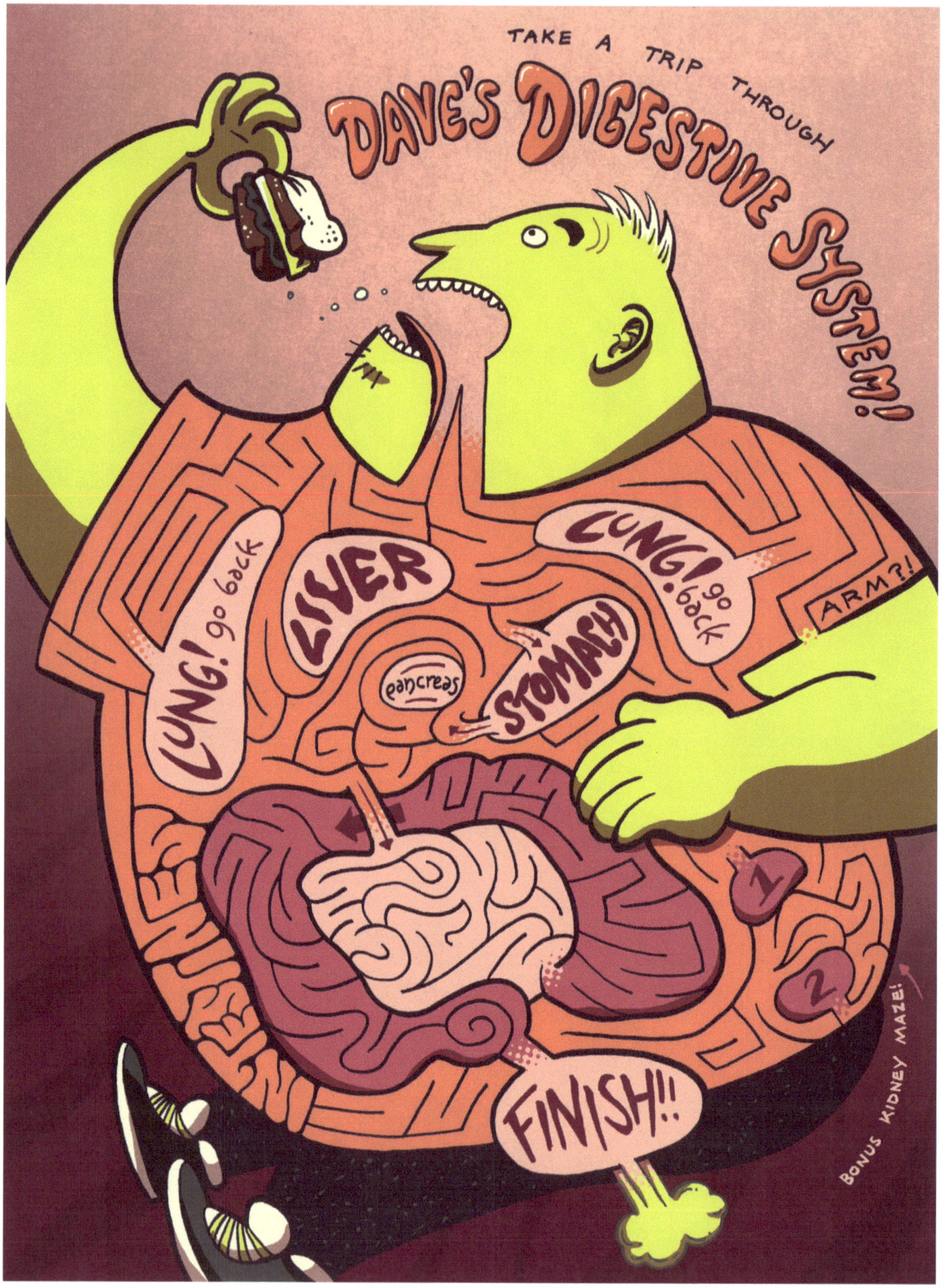

Dave's Digestive System
Dorian Lafferre

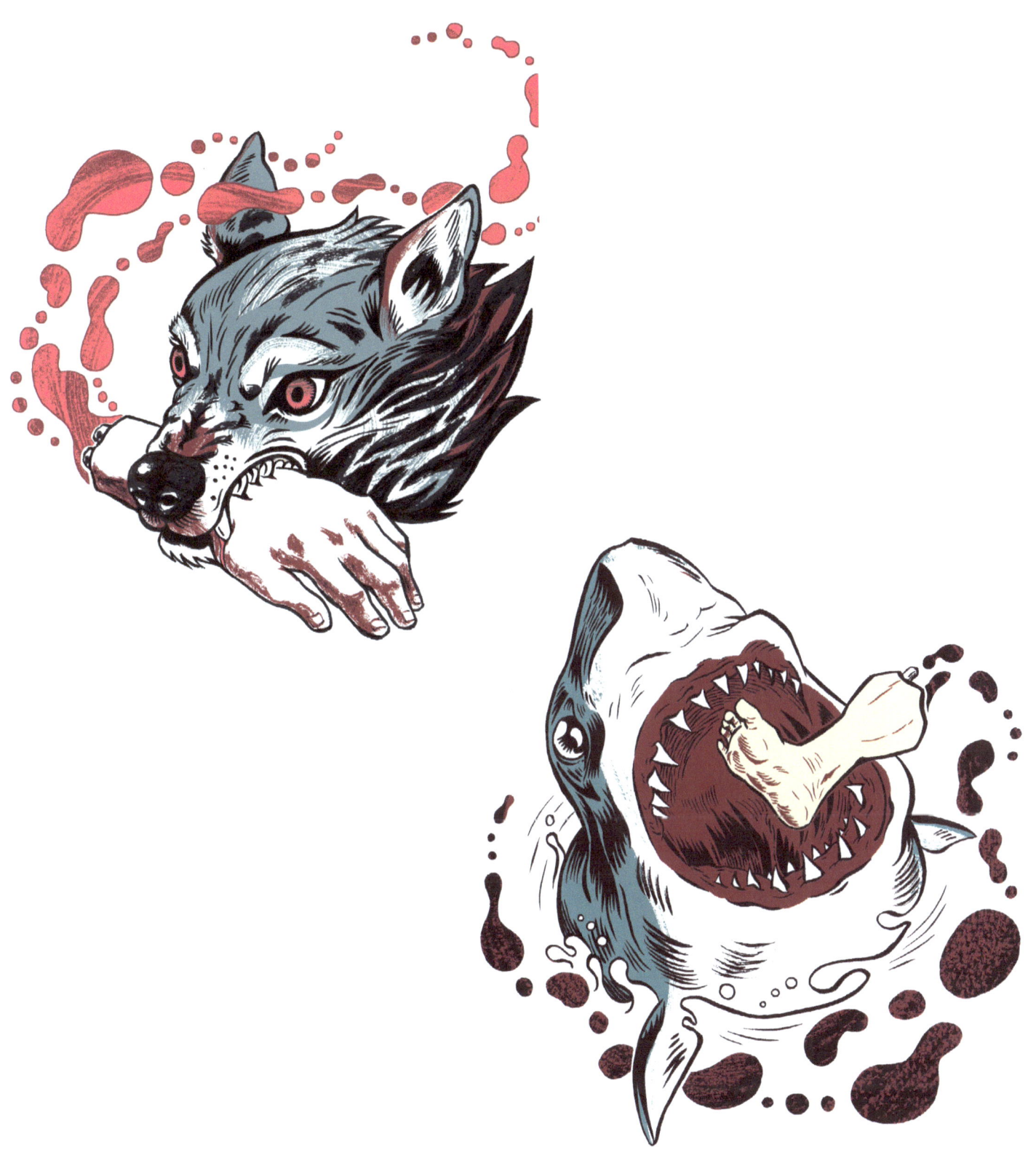

Gray Wolf (left) Great White(right)
Dorian Lafferre

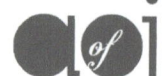

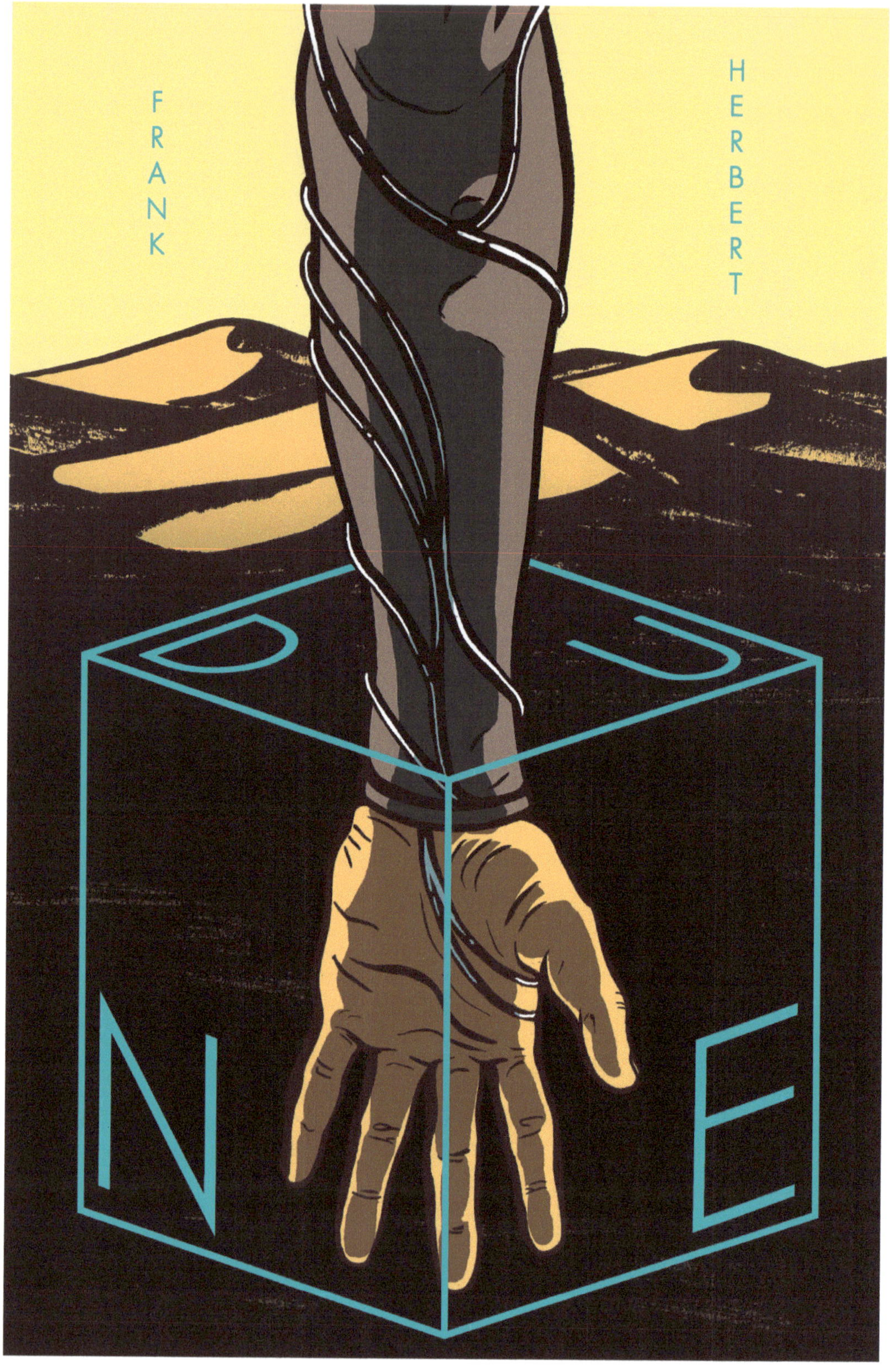

Dune
Dorian Lafferre

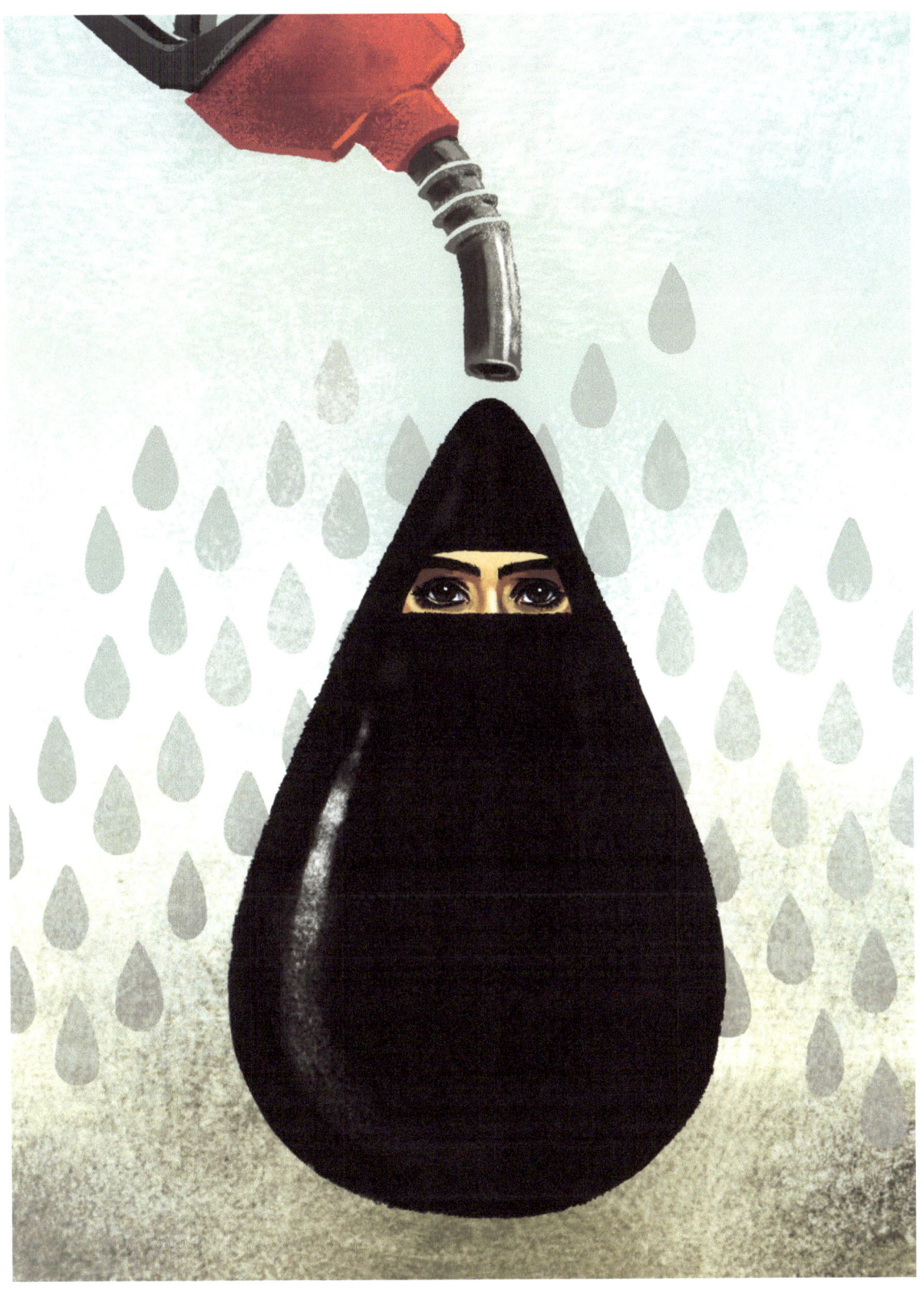

Women and Oil
Colleen Clark

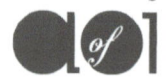

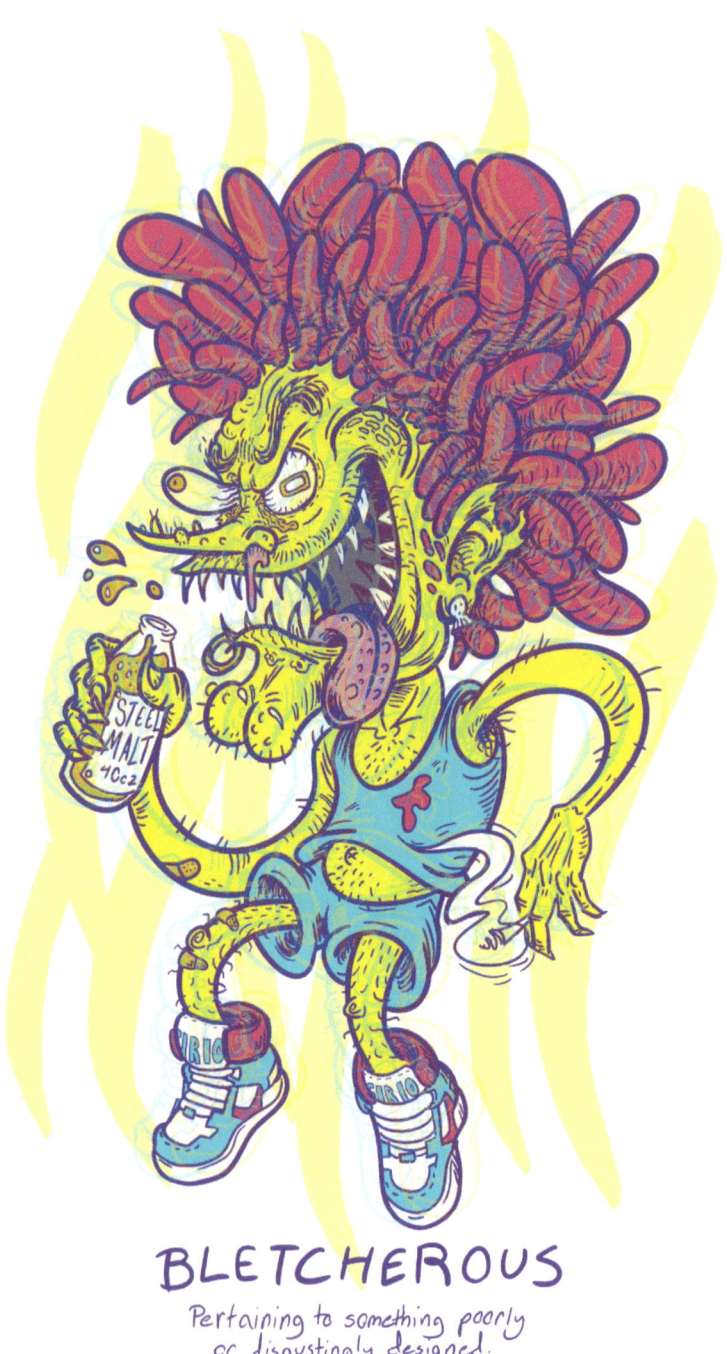

Bletcherous
Andrew Peña

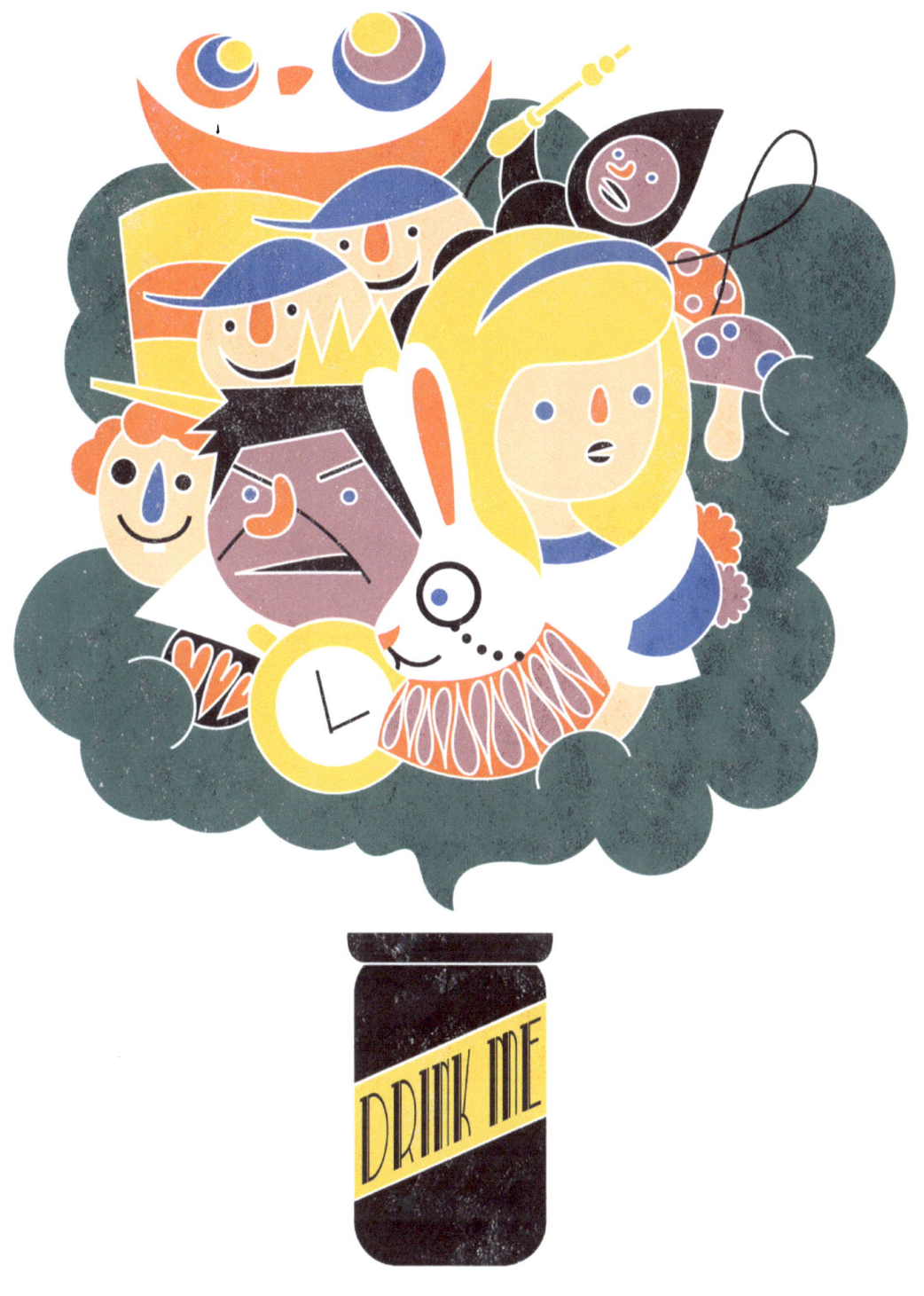

Alice in Wonderland I
Sophie Lim

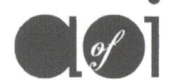

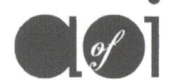

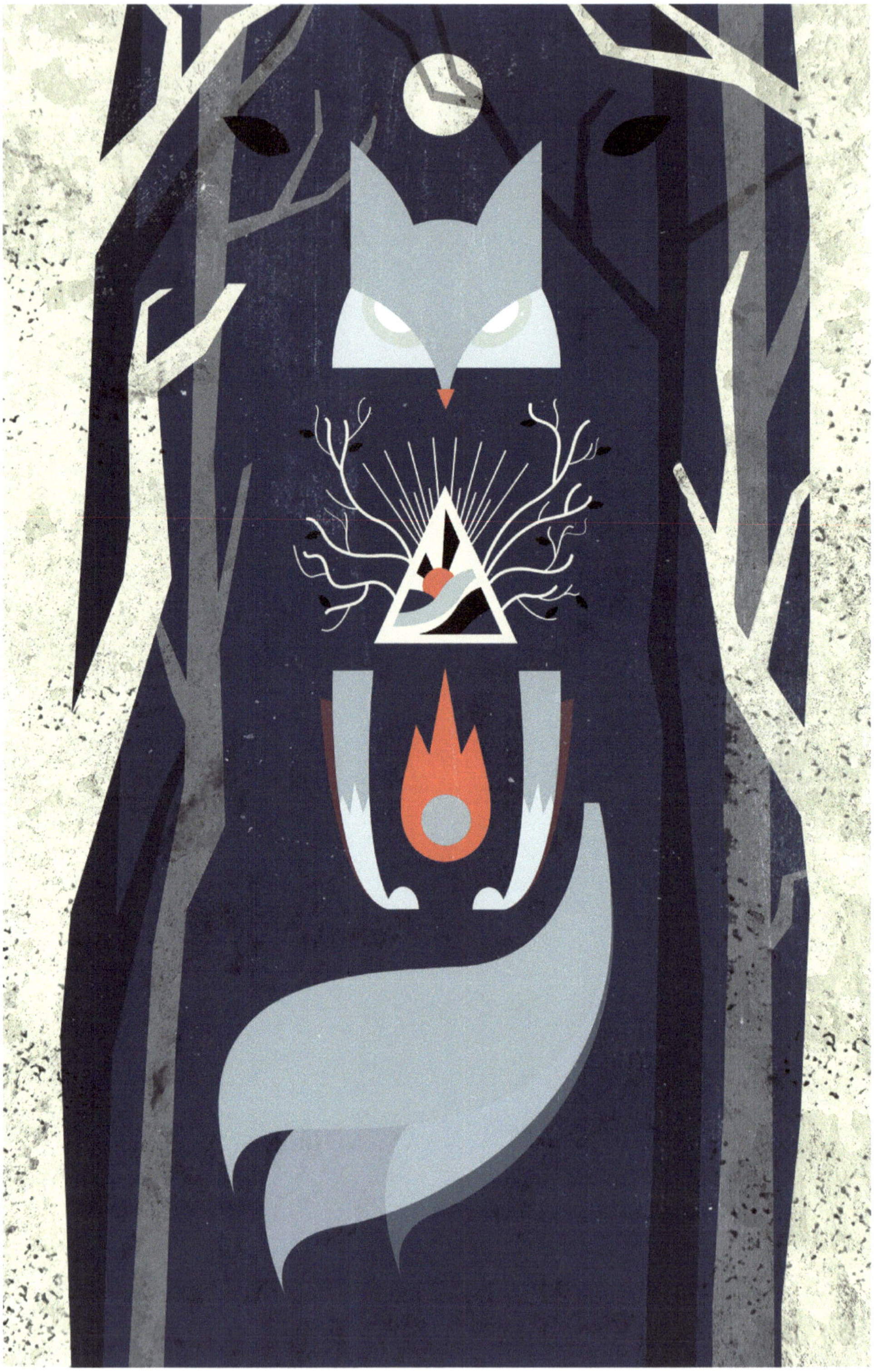

Fox
Sophie Lim

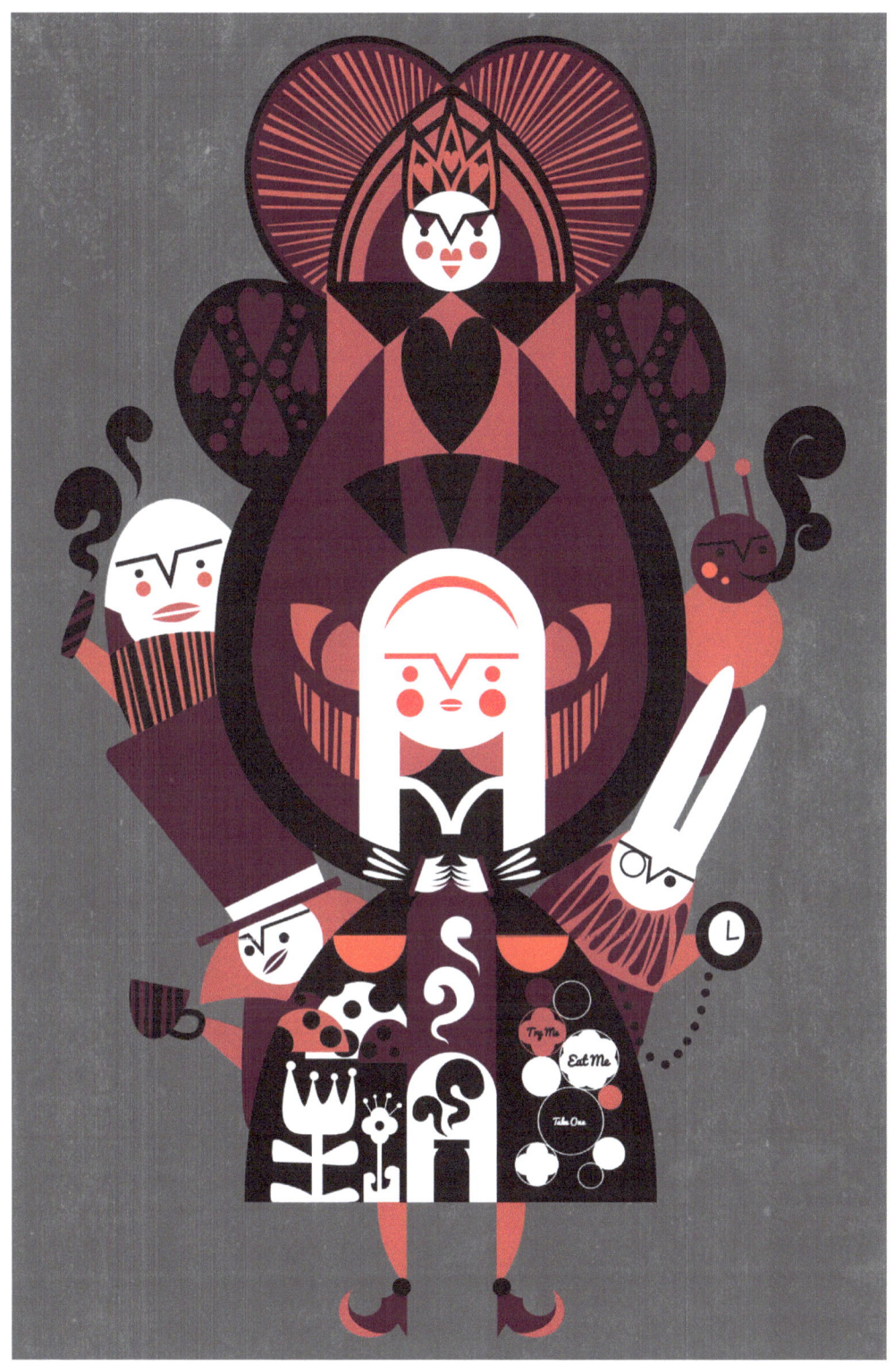

Alice in Wonderland II
Sophie Lim

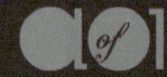

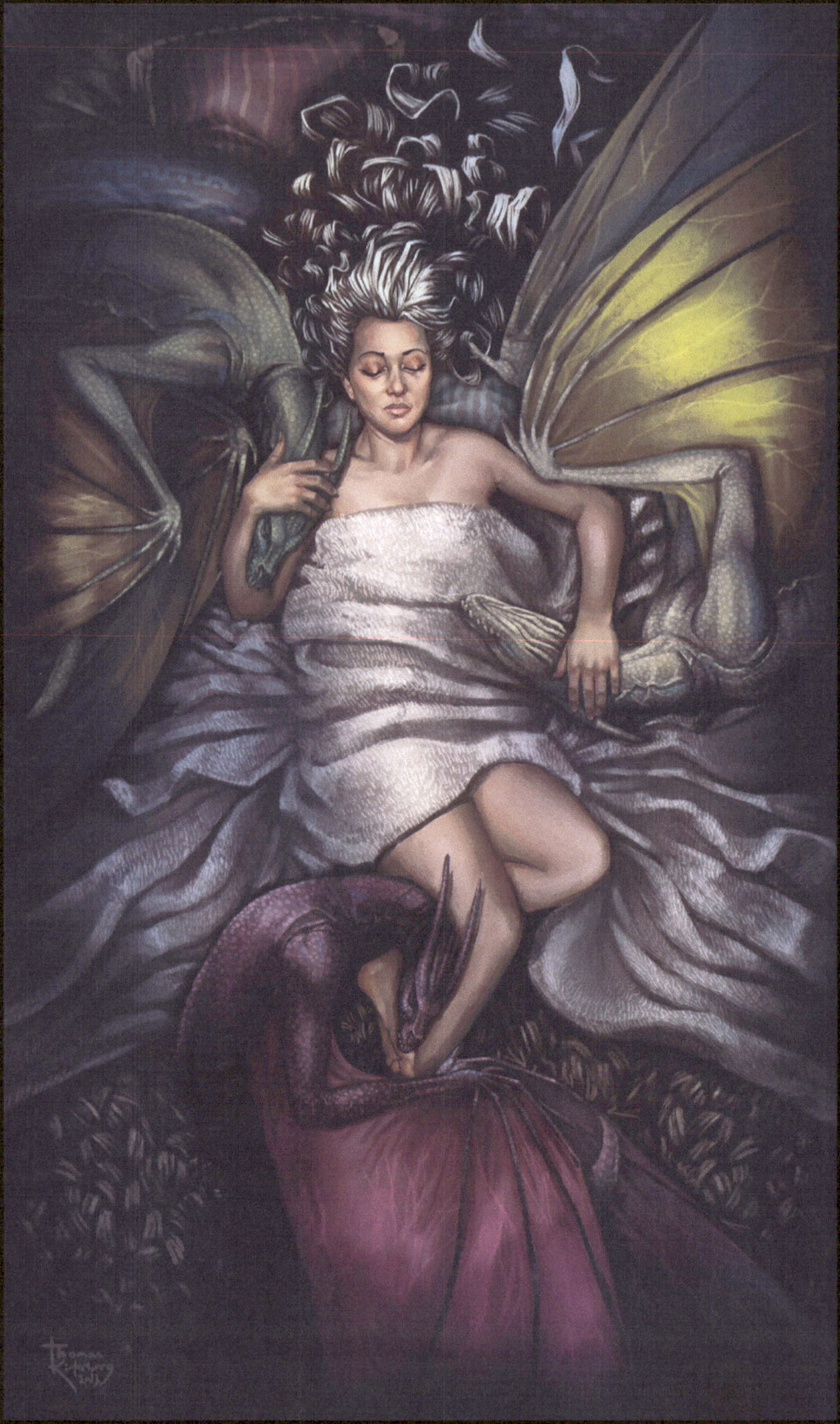

1ST PLACE WINNER

Mother of Dragons
Thomas Kirkeberg

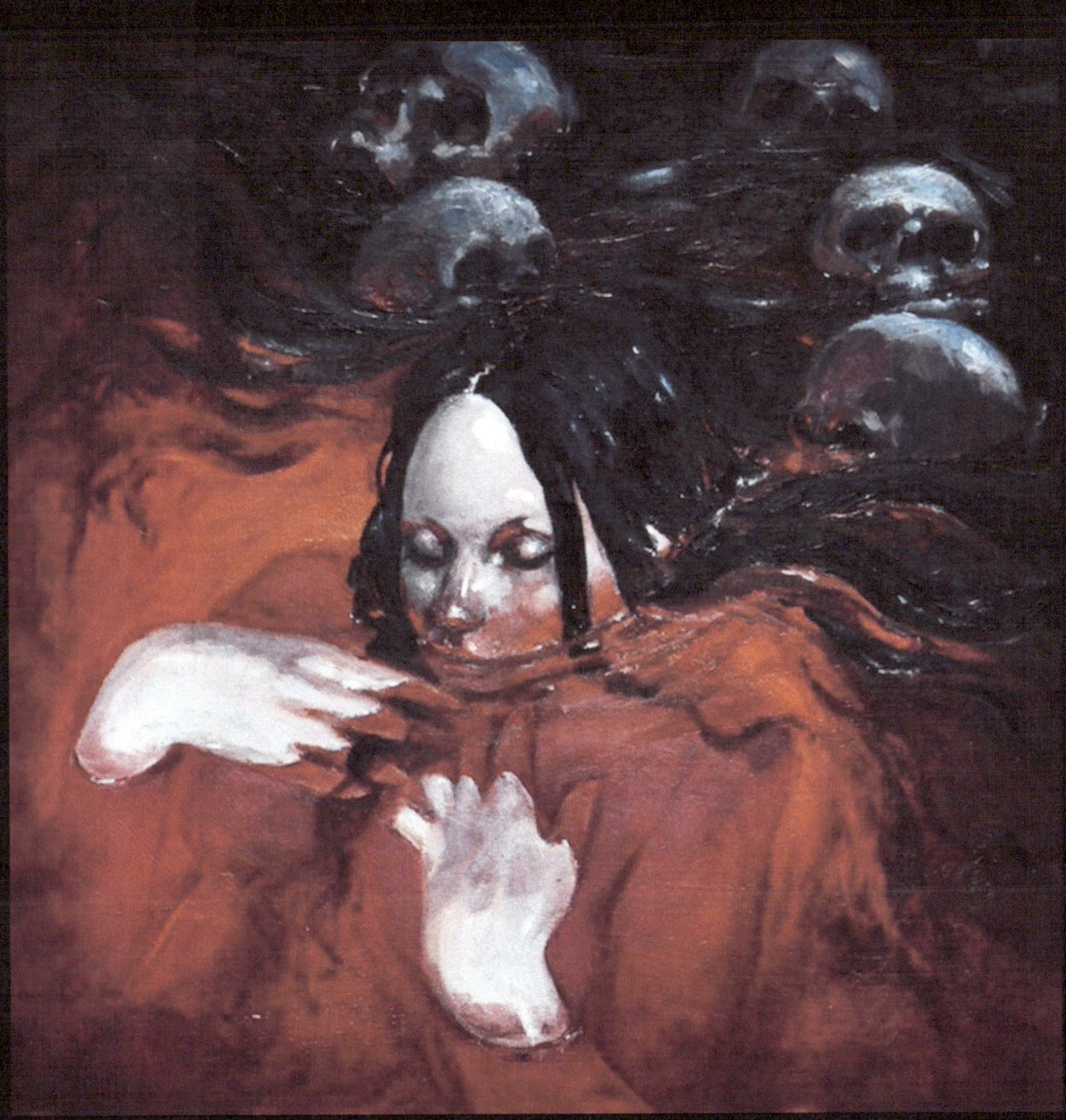

2ND PLACE WINNER

KRYSTI KALKMAN JUDGE'S PICK

Elizabeth Bathory
Josh Parkinson

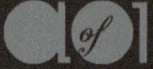

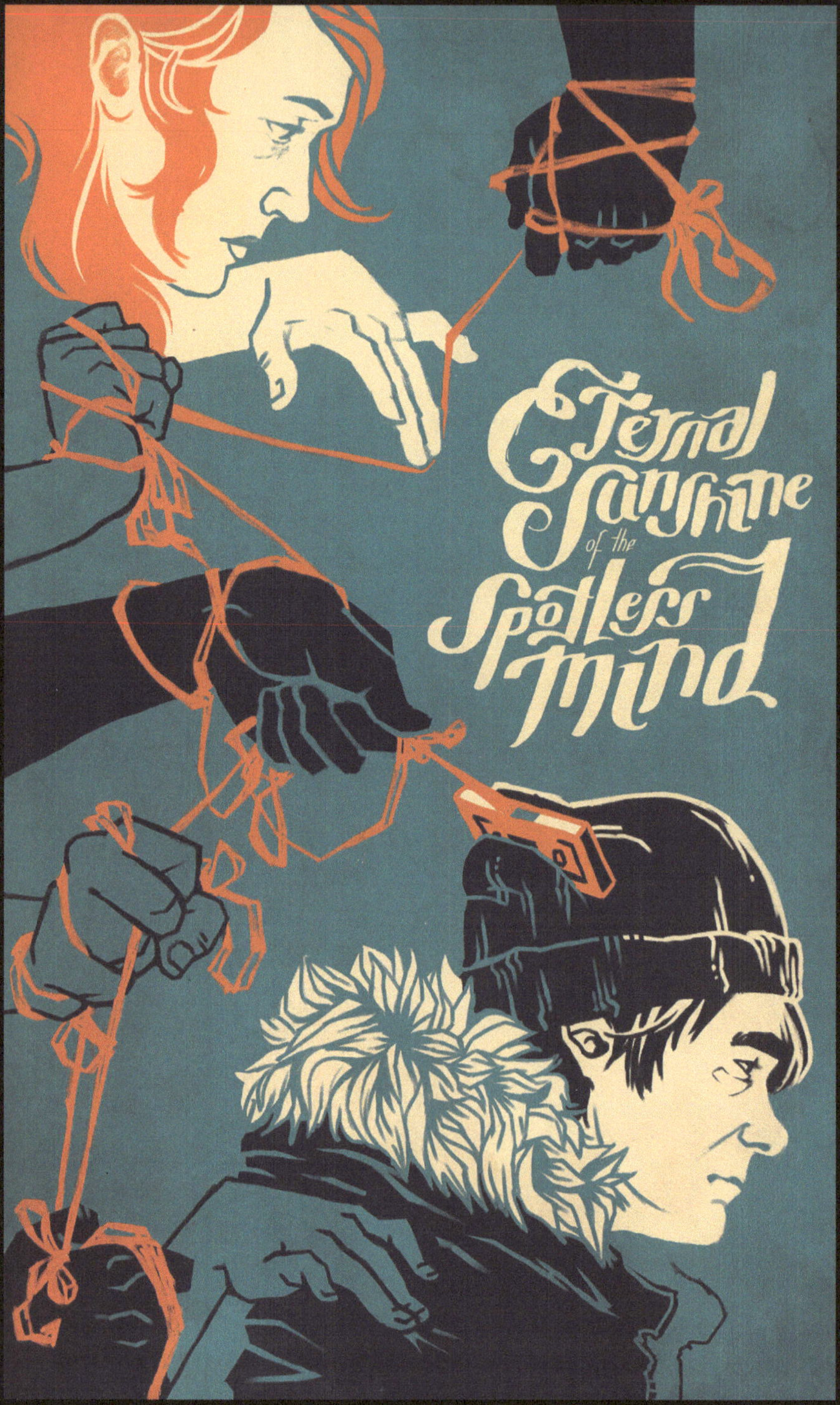

3RD PLACE WINNER

JEREMY SLAGLE JUDGE'S PICK

Eternal Sunshine Of The Spotless Mind
Emmett Shearer

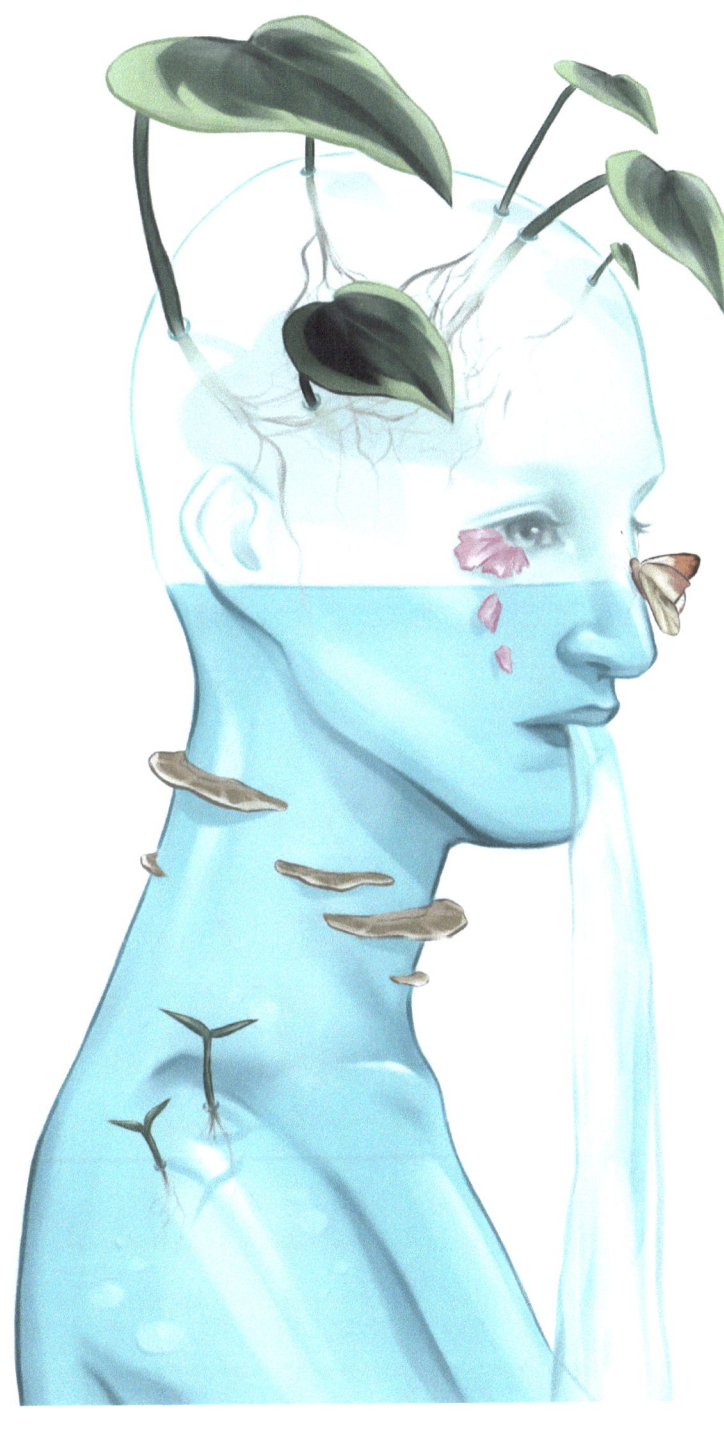

Simple Thoughts
Pornpin Cecchini

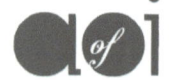

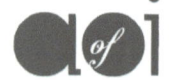

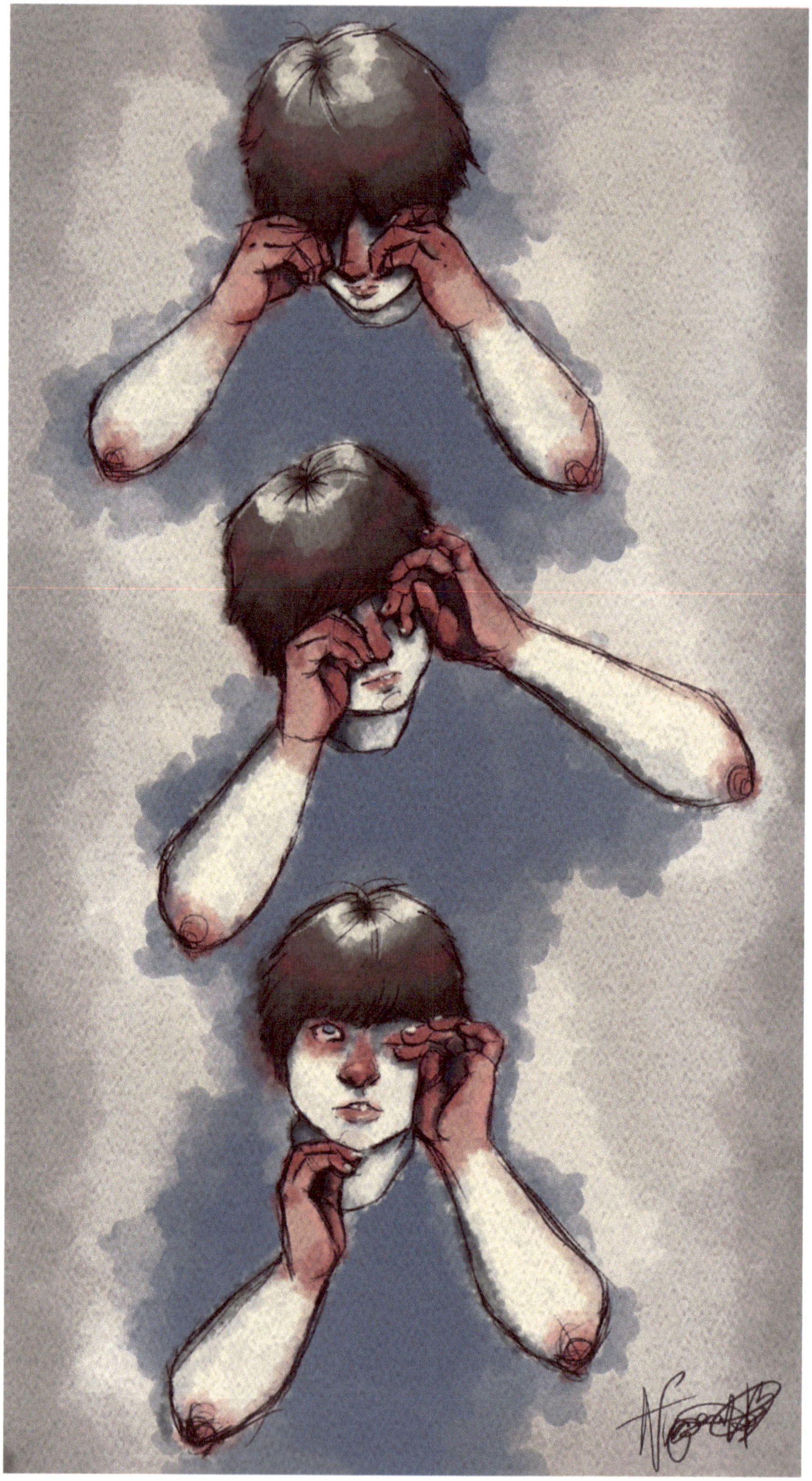

Itchy Eyes
Anna Vigorito

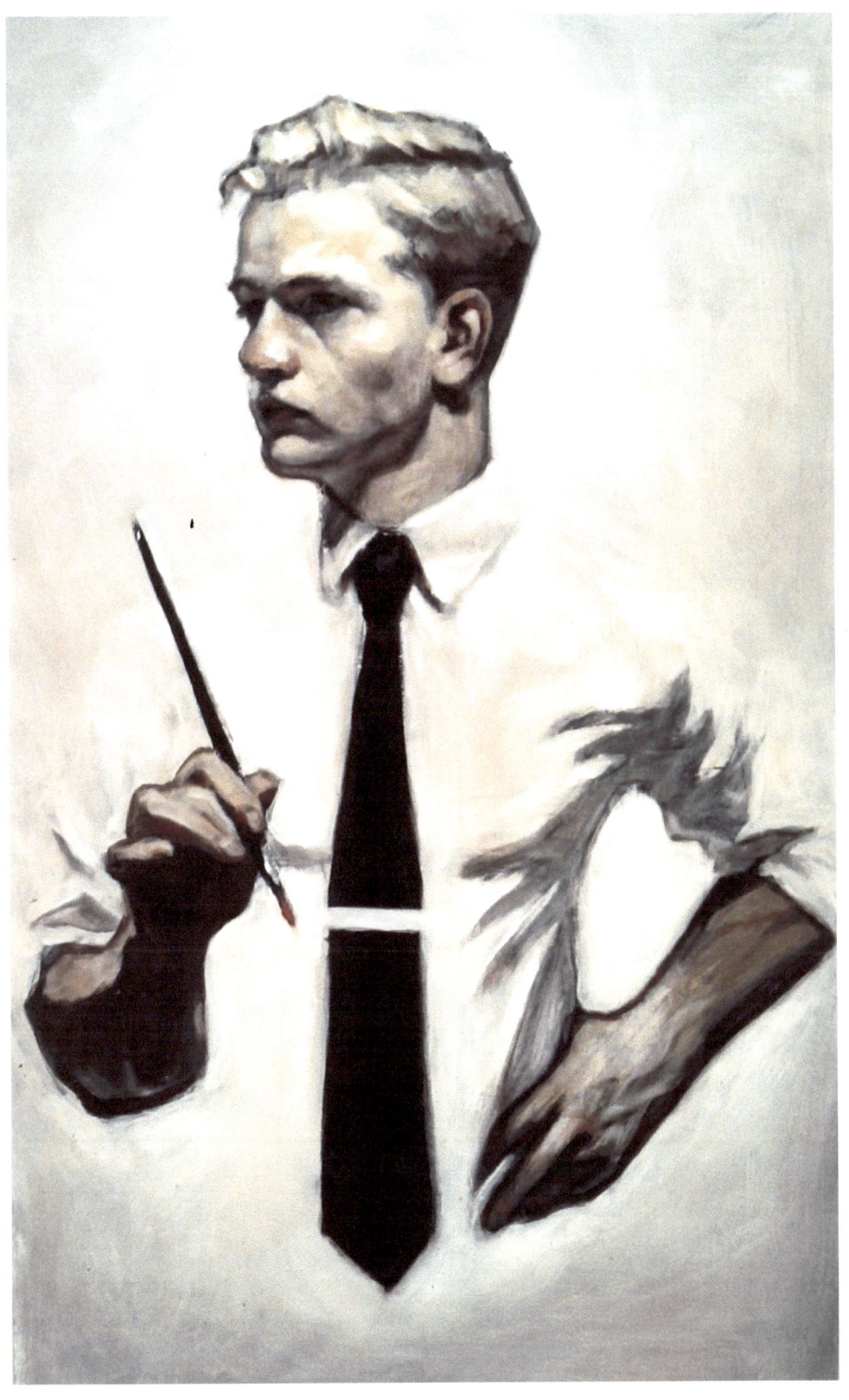

Self Portrait
Josh Parkinson

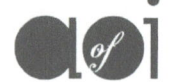

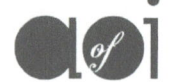

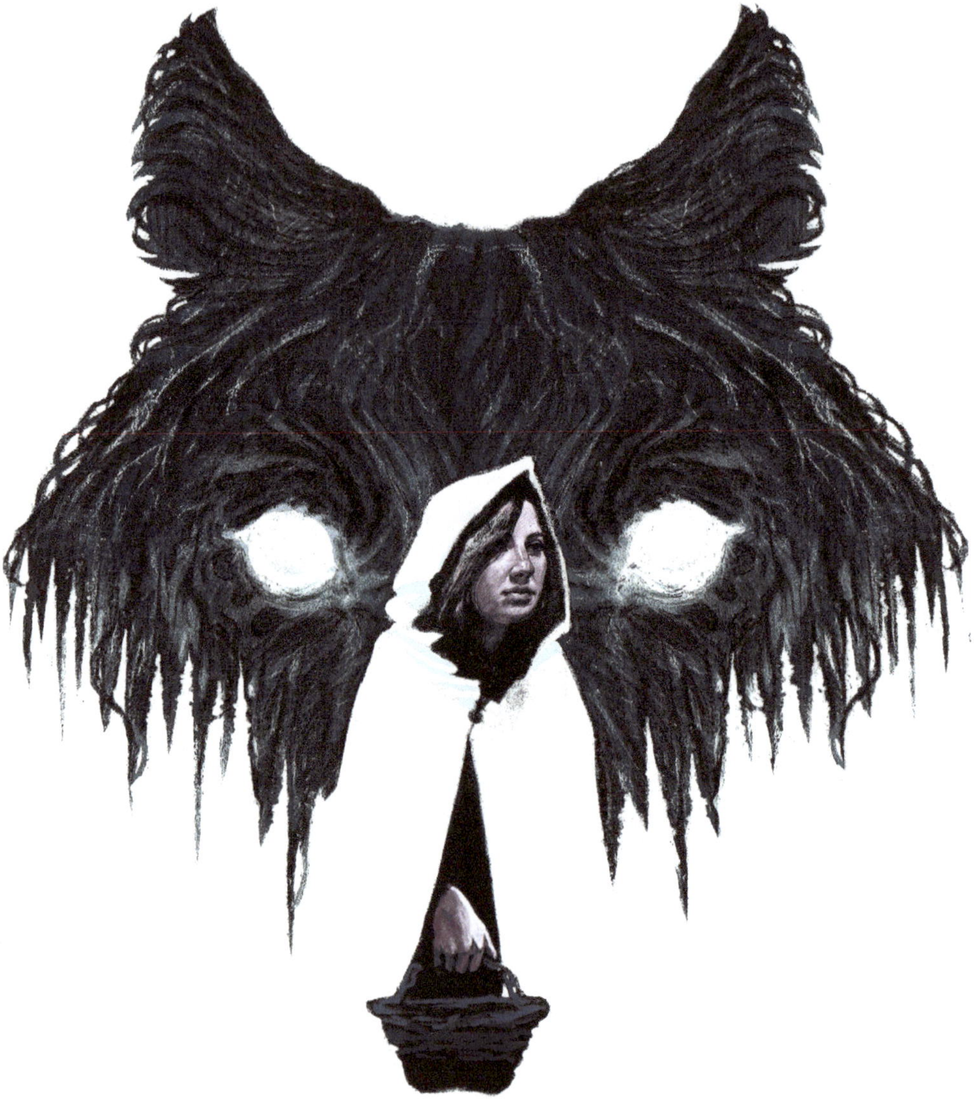

Wolf
Josh Parkinson

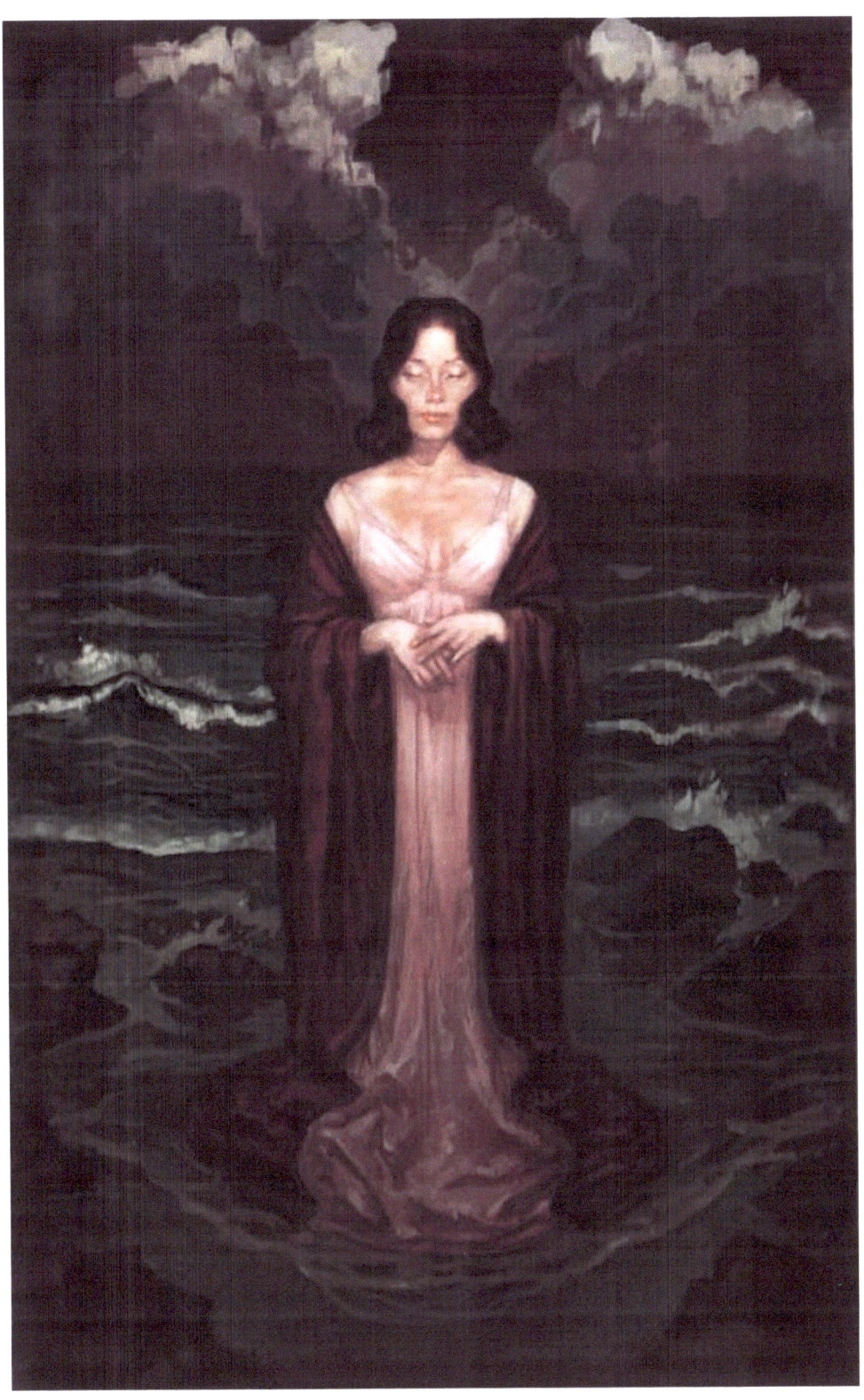

Mercedes
Josh Parkinson

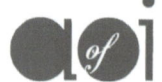

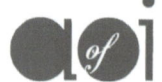

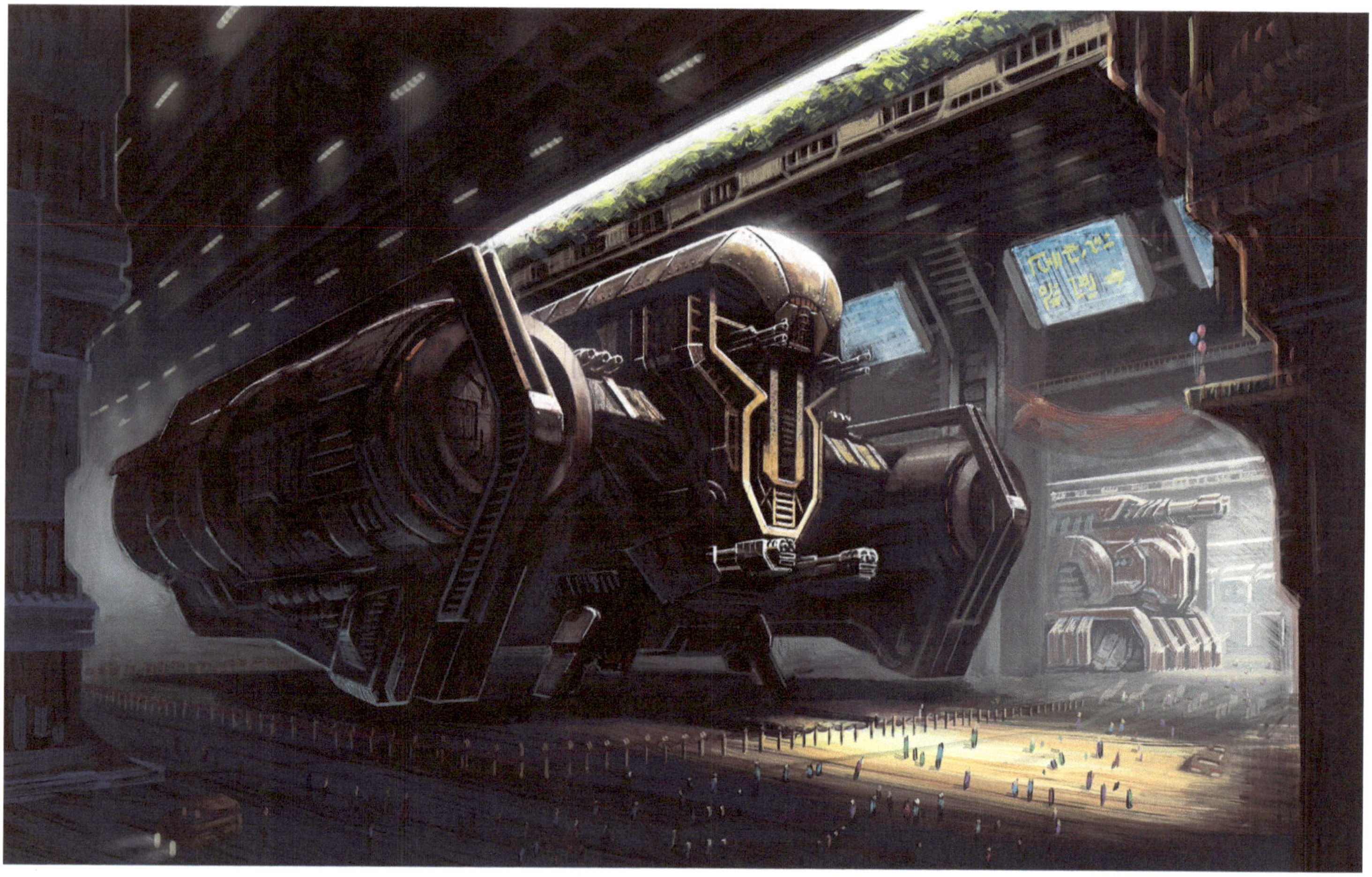

War Museum
Alex Kim

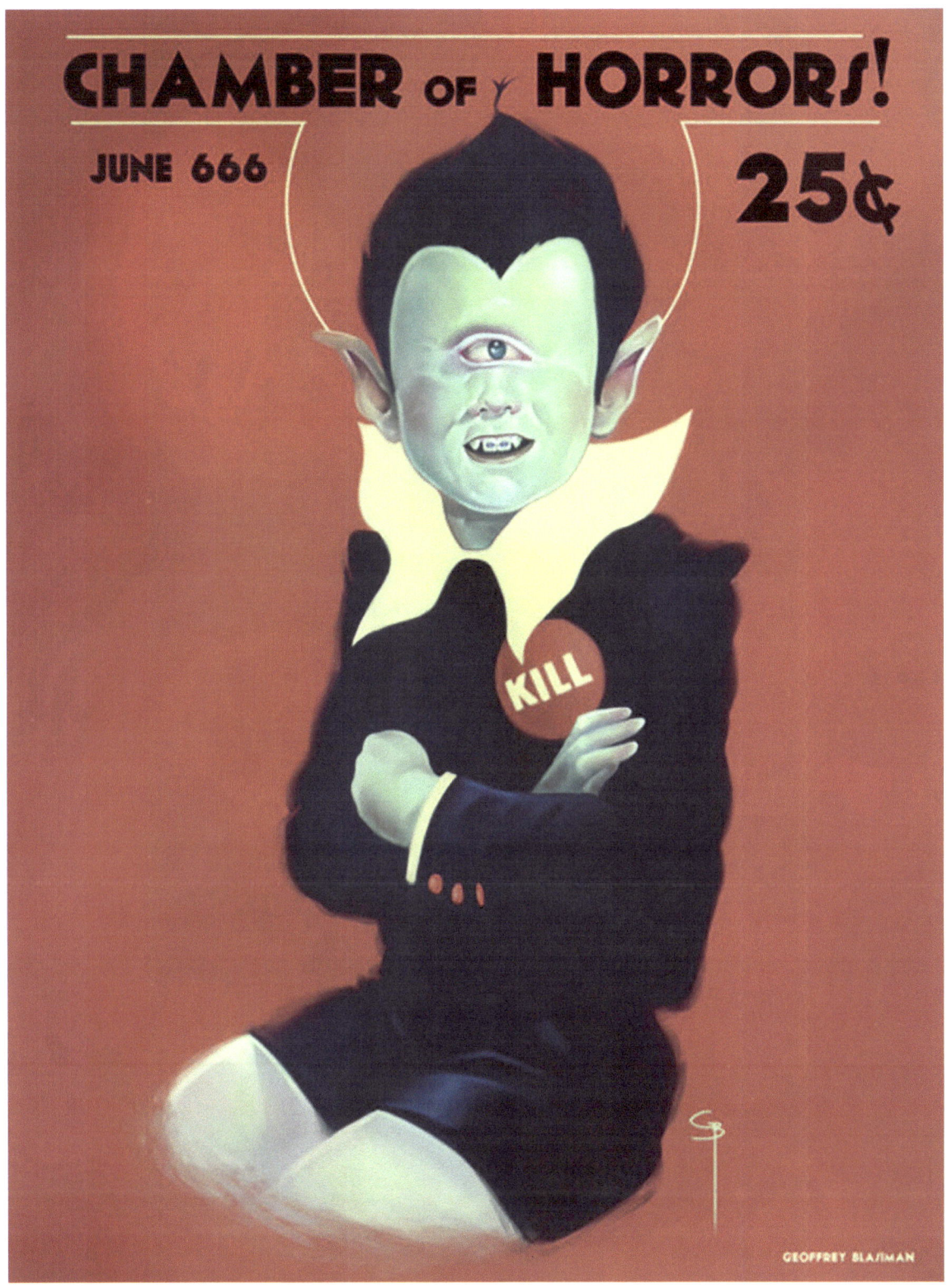

Chamber of Horrors
Geoffrey Blasiman

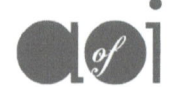

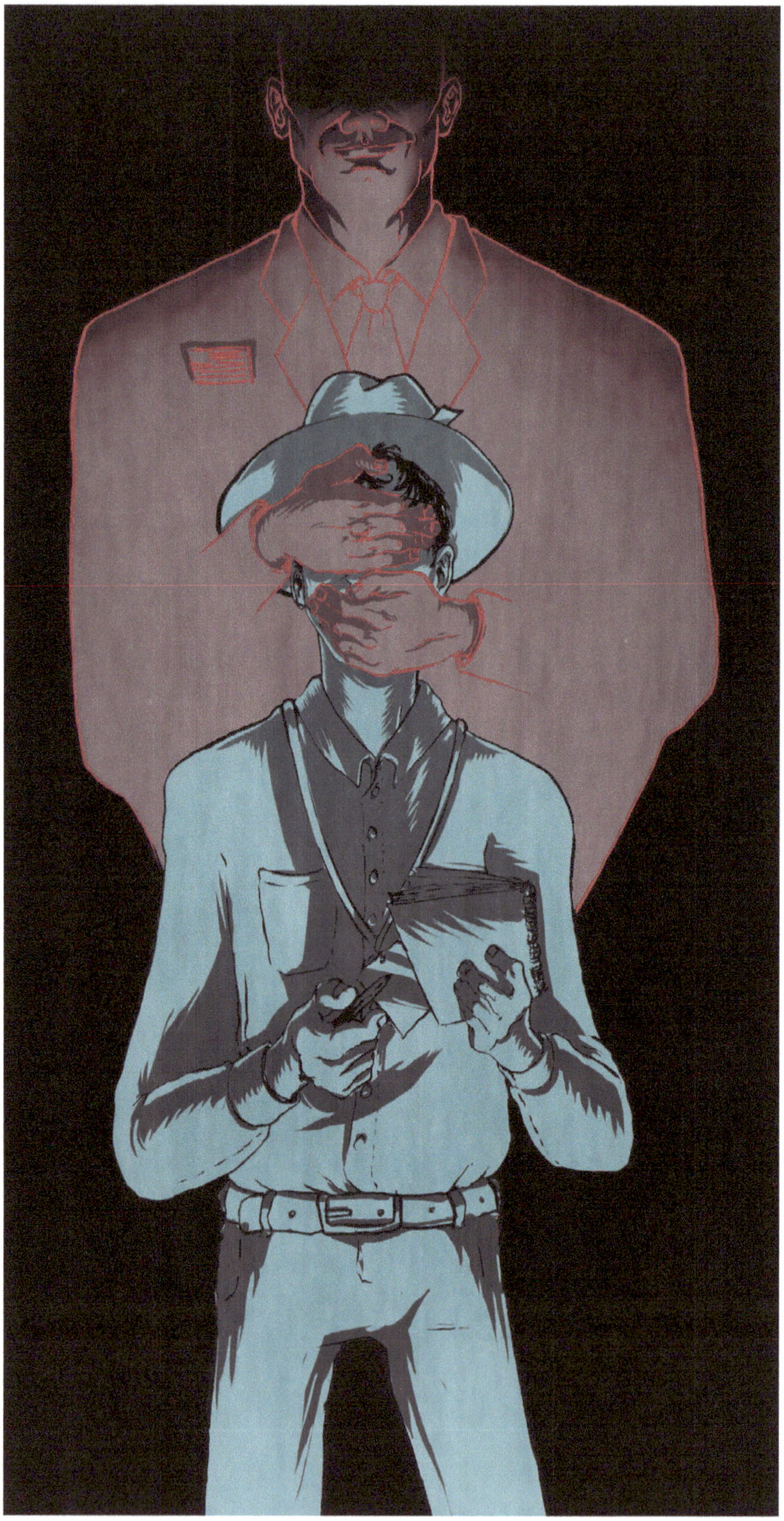

Just Politics
Hannah Ploechl

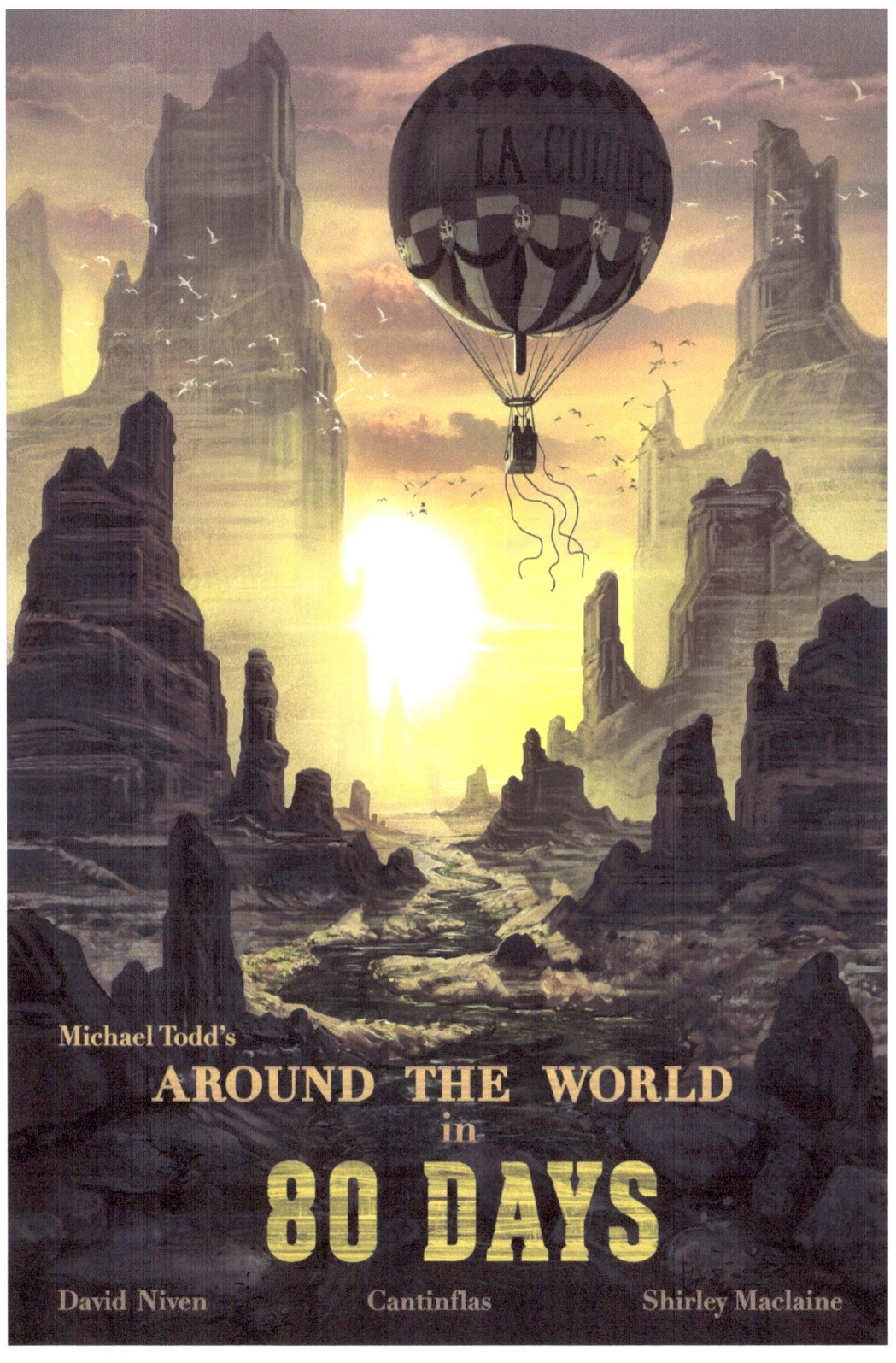

Around The World In 80 Days
Erlson Neba

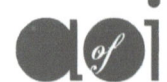

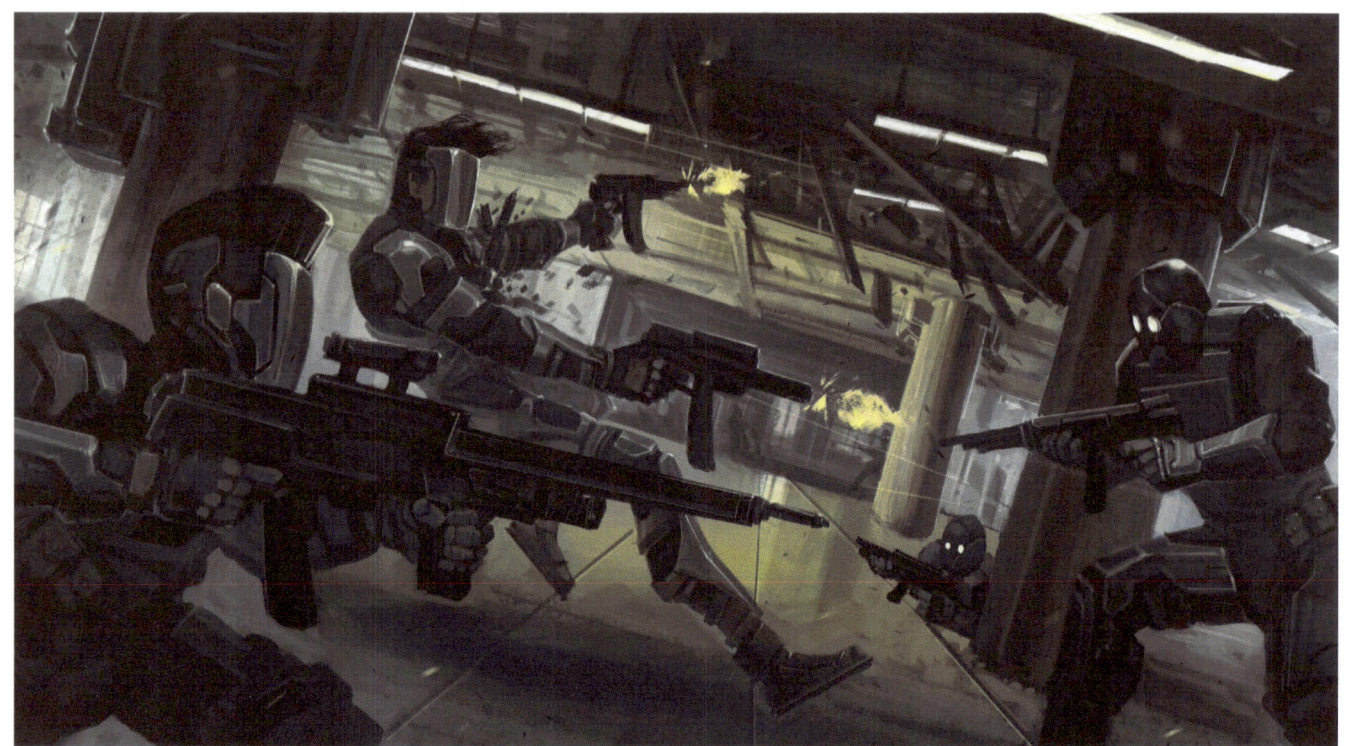

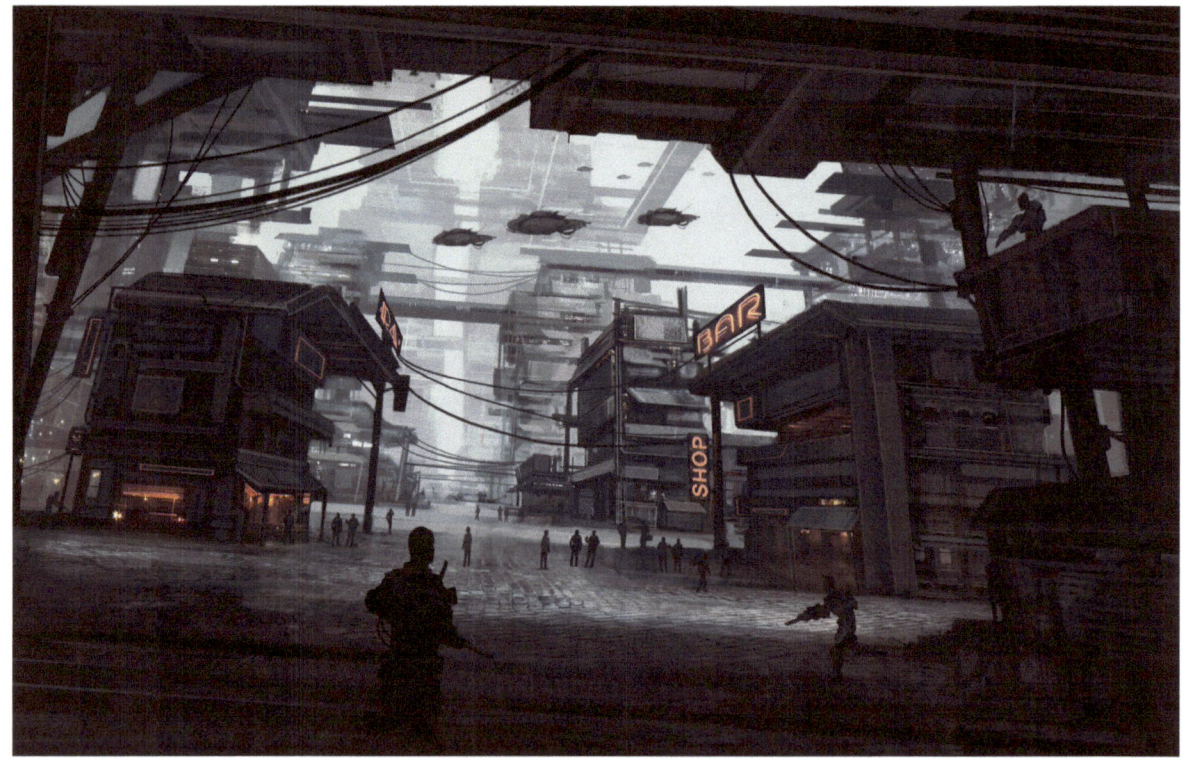

Chaos (Upper) The Market (Bottom)
Erlson Neba

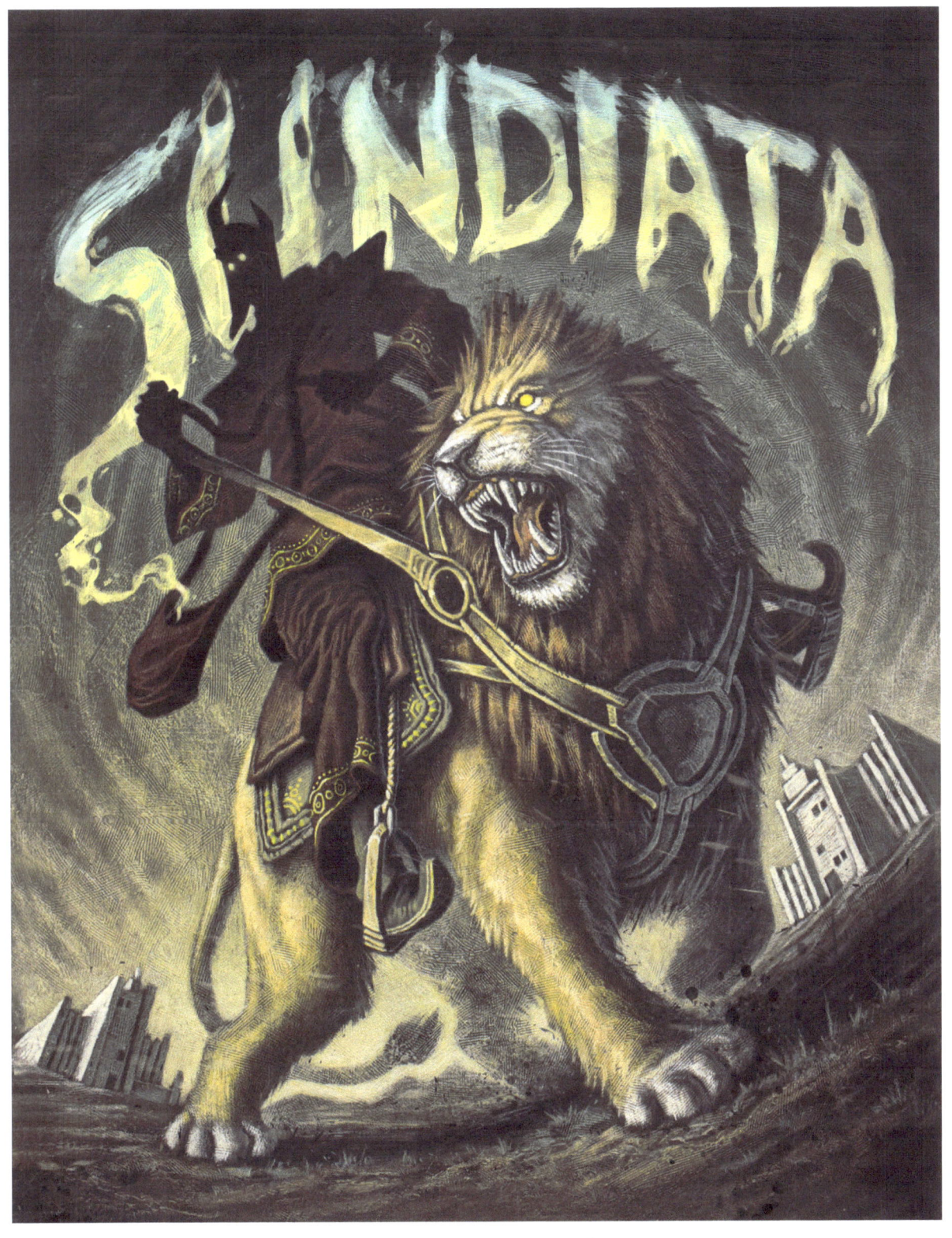

DANA MARTIN RYAN JUDGE'S PICK

Sundiata
Erlson Neba

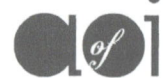

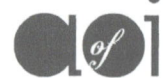

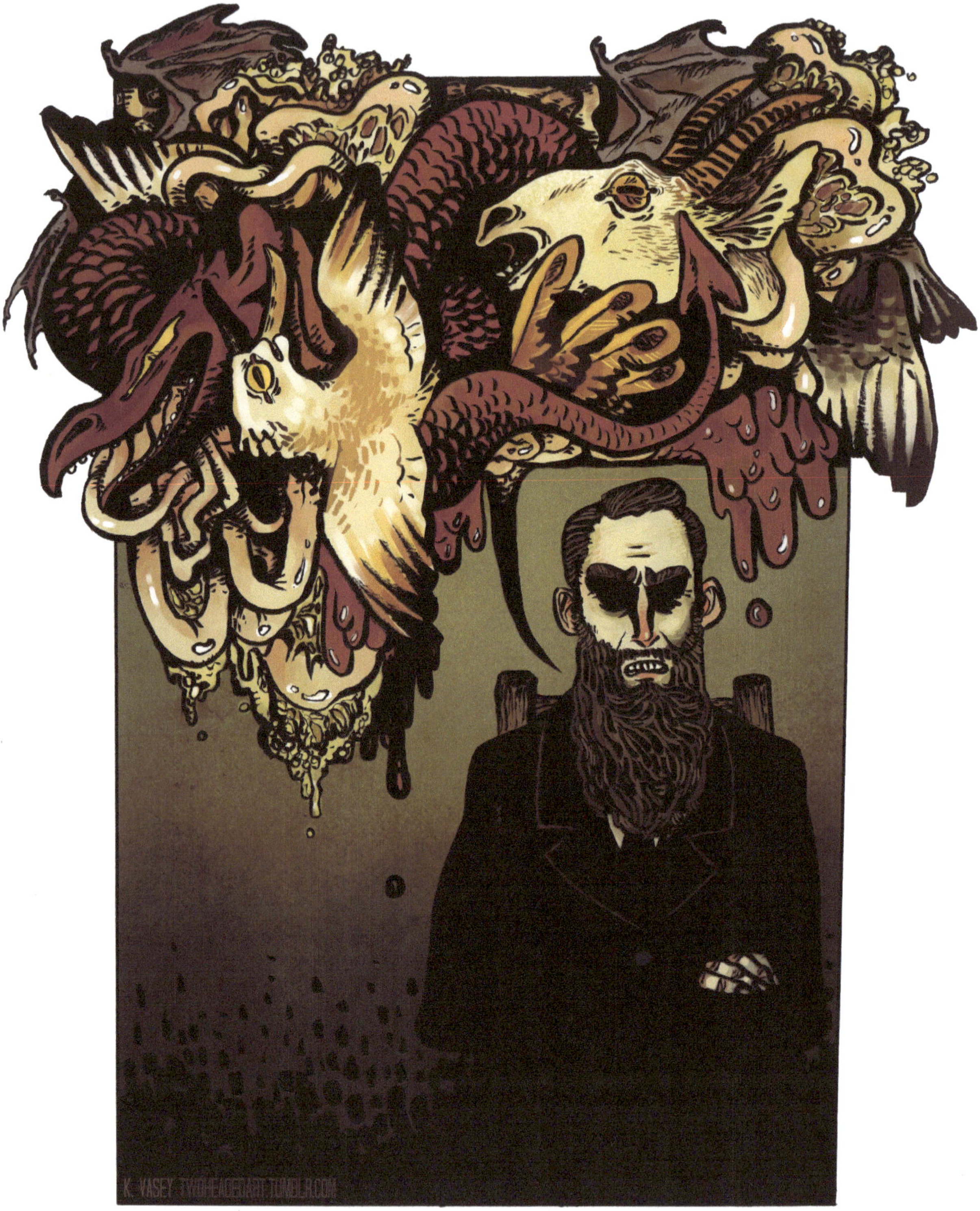

Lyssophobia
Katie Vasey

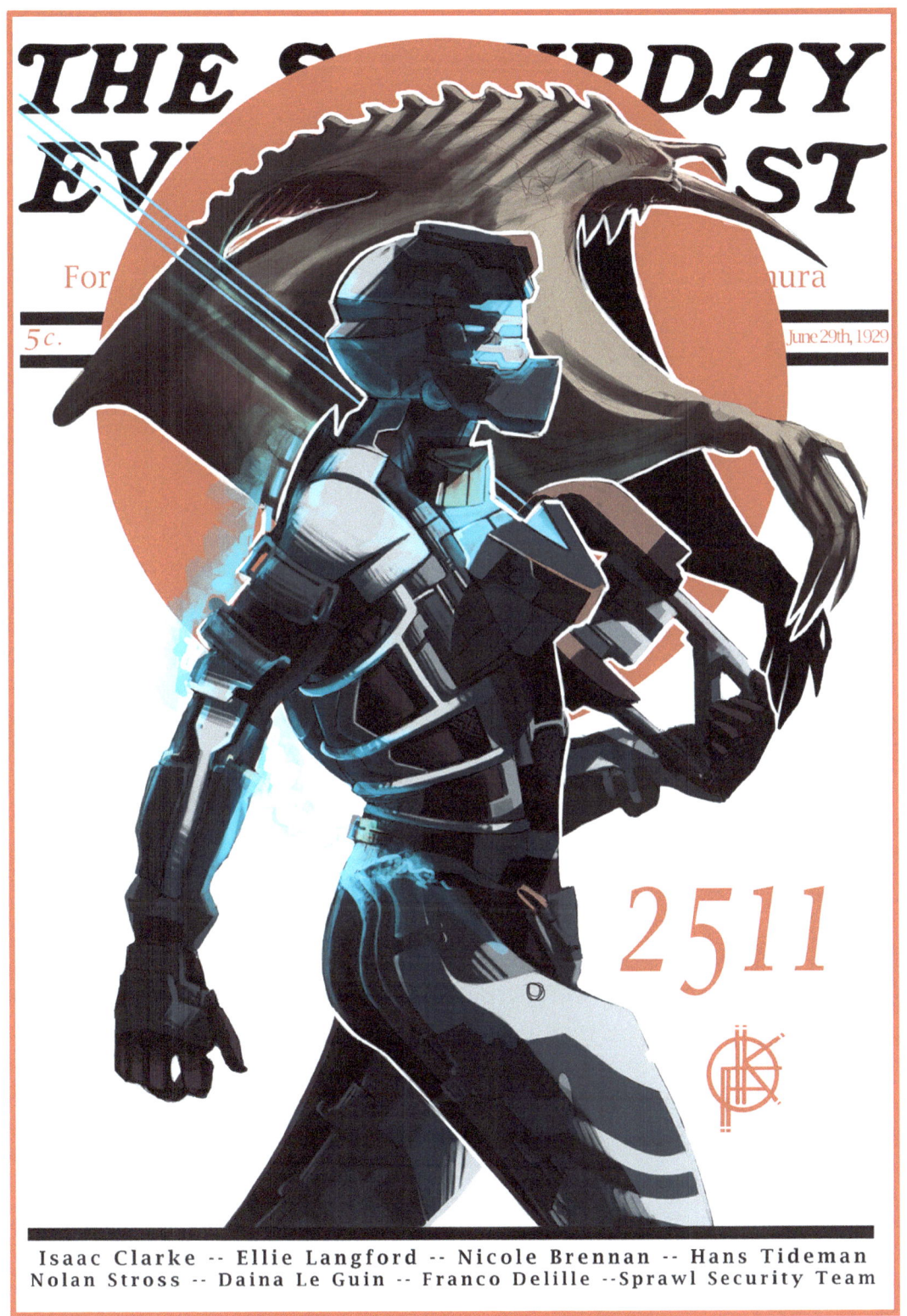

Saturday Evening Post Dead Space
Katherine Fedorco

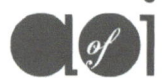

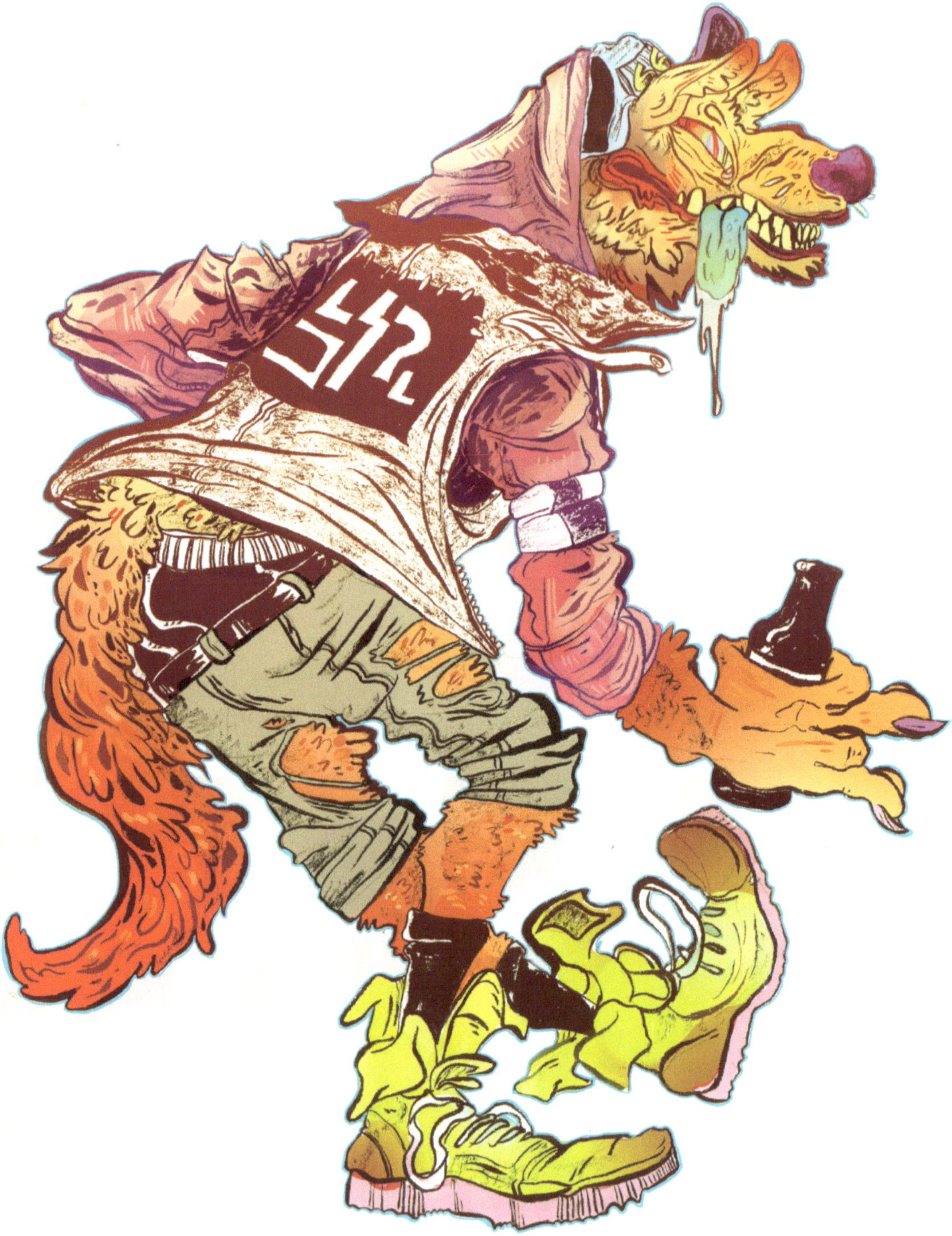

The Harvest
Kristen Starlein

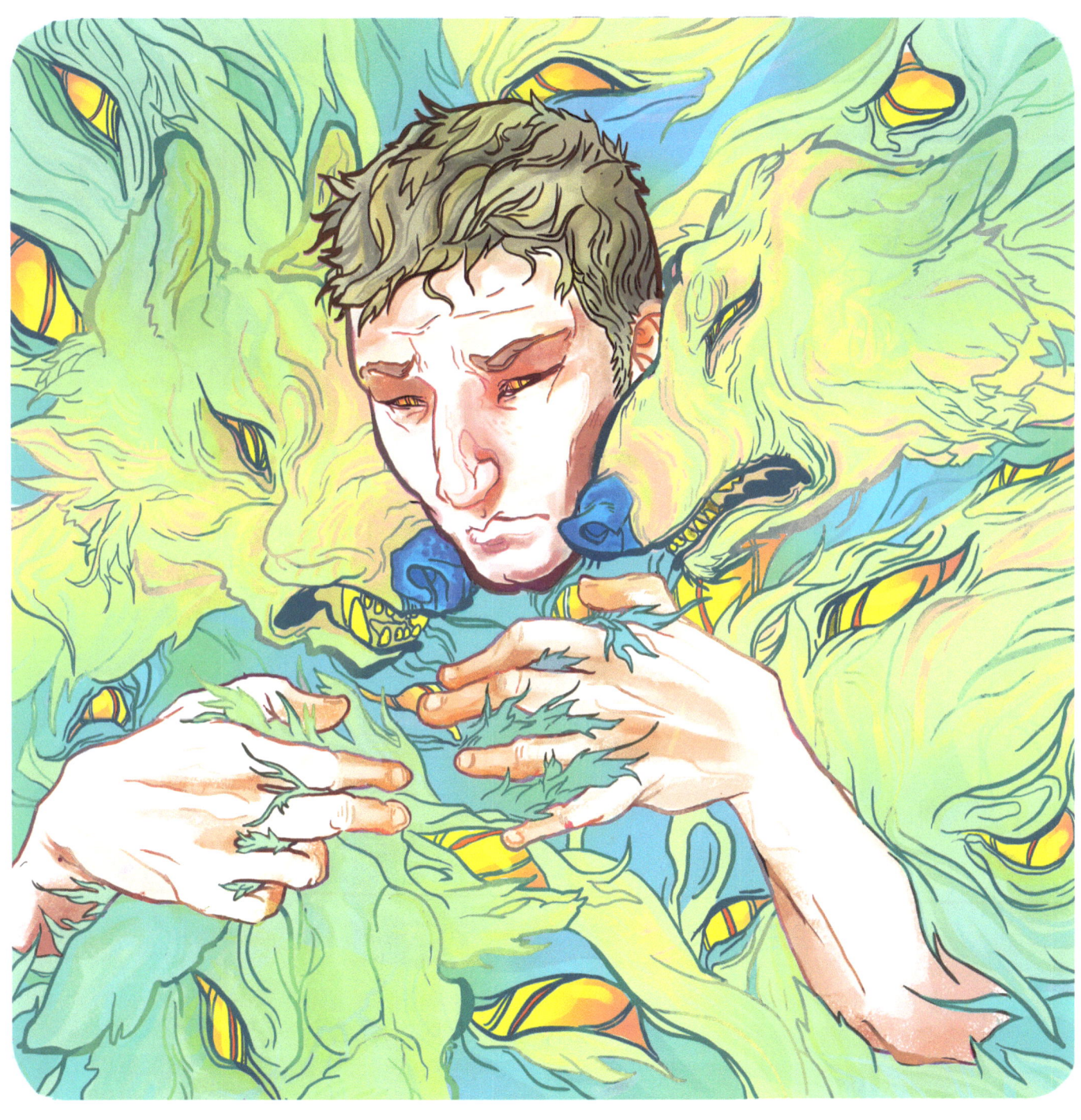

Too Late
Kristen Starlein

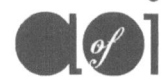

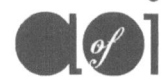

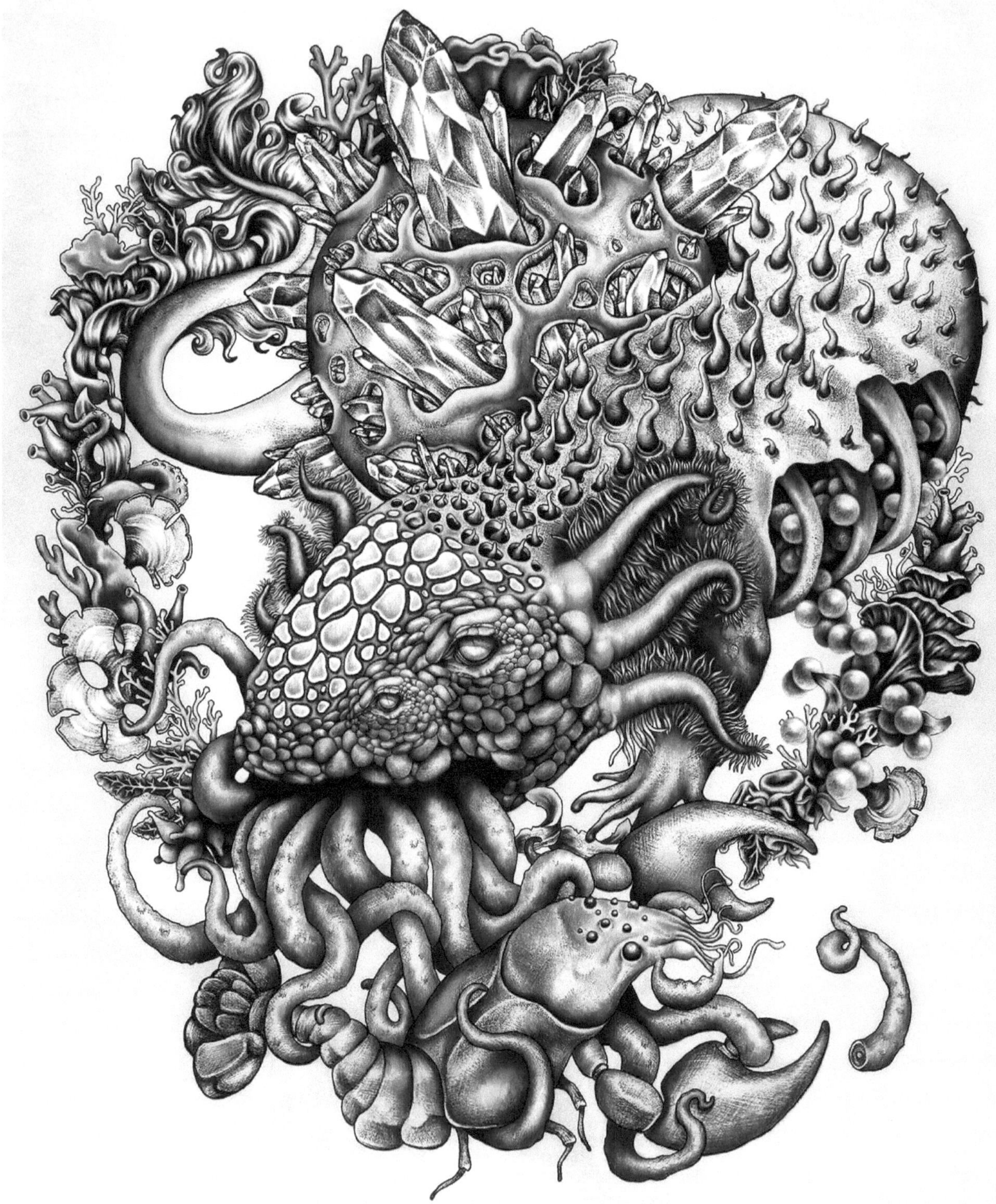

Hollow Moon
Kit Elizabeth Mizeres

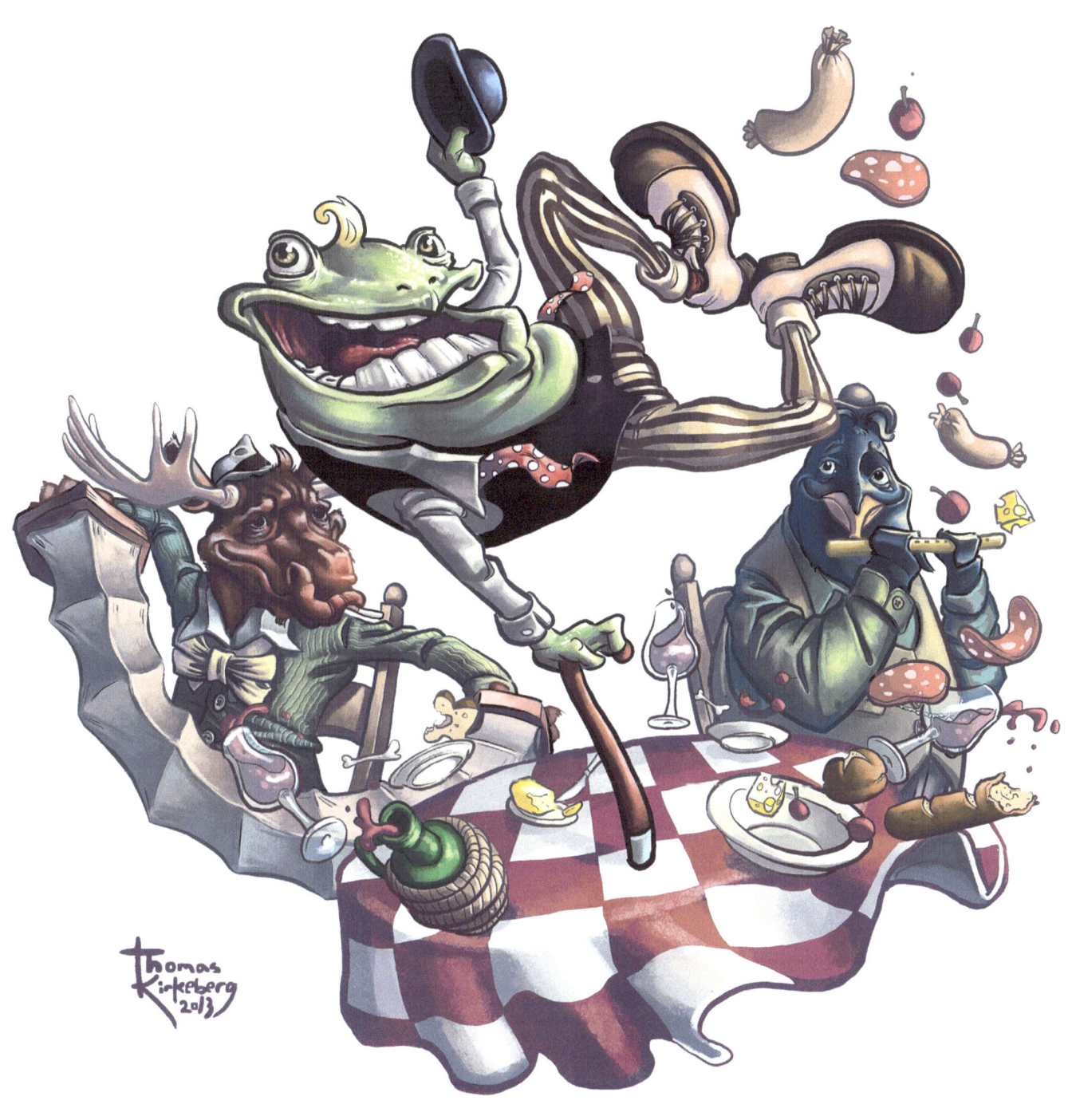

Frog On The Table
Thomas Kirkeberg

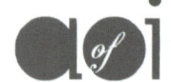

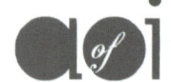

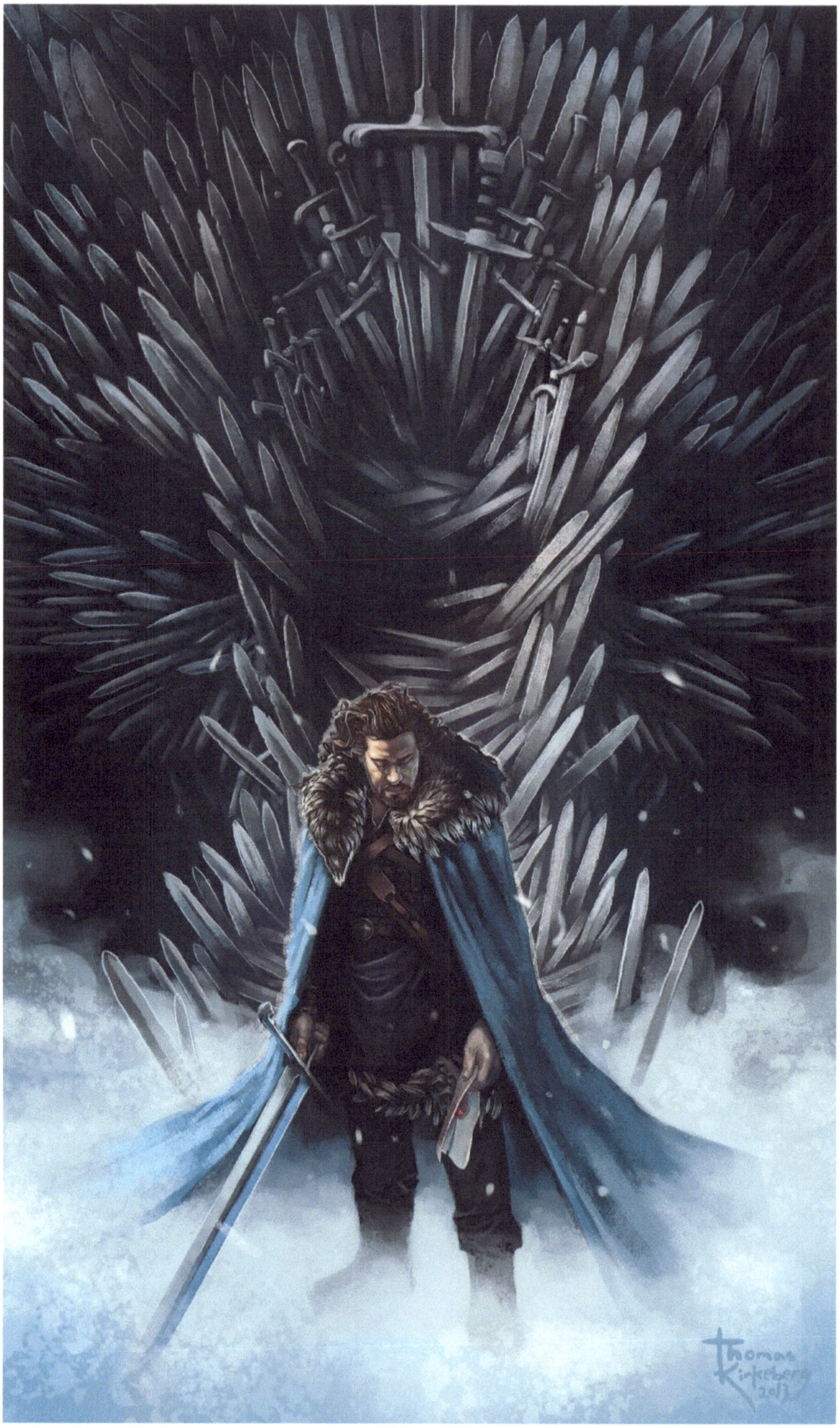

Winter Is Coming
Thomas Kirkeberg

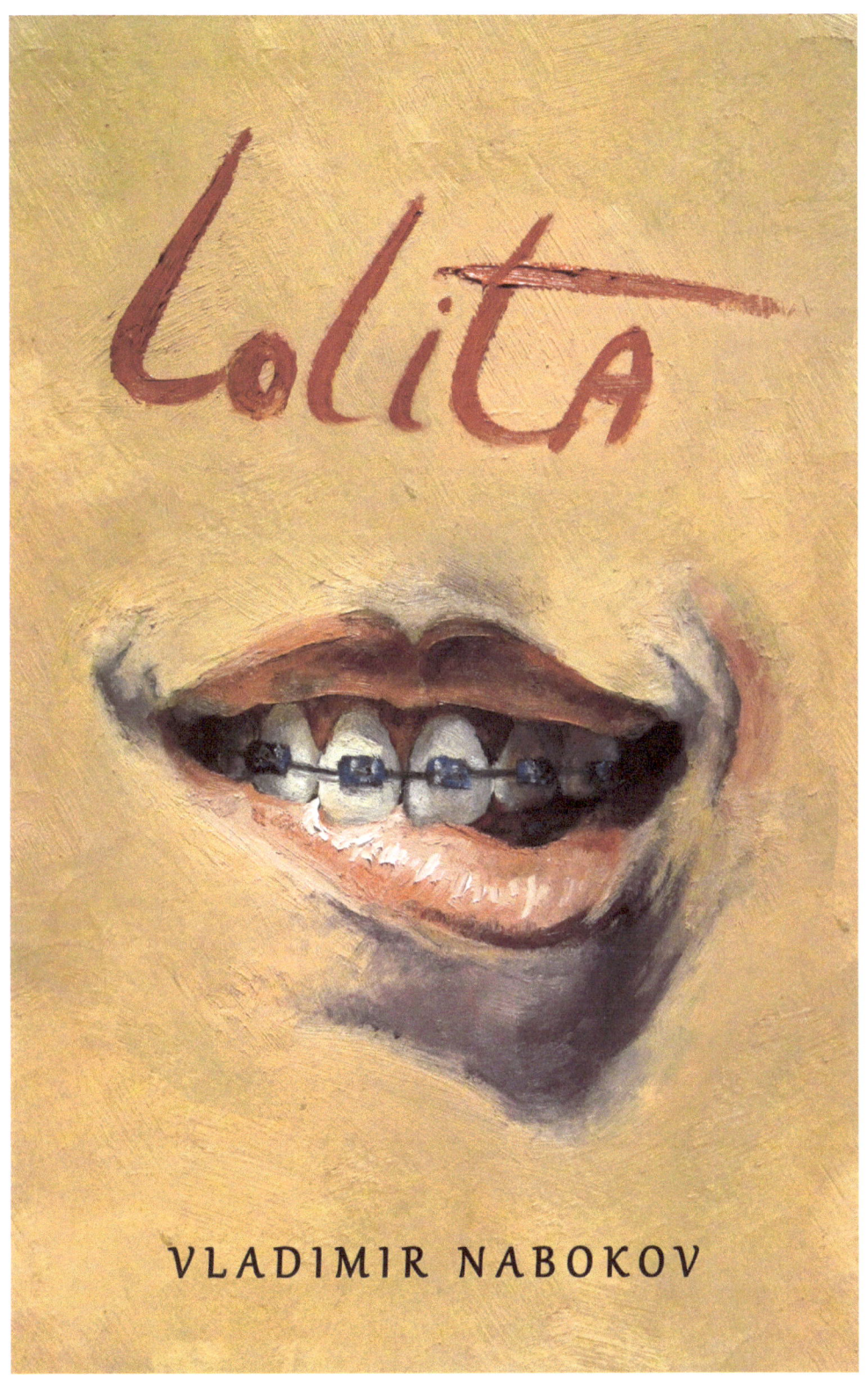

Lolita
Sarah Buzzard

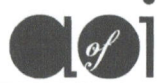

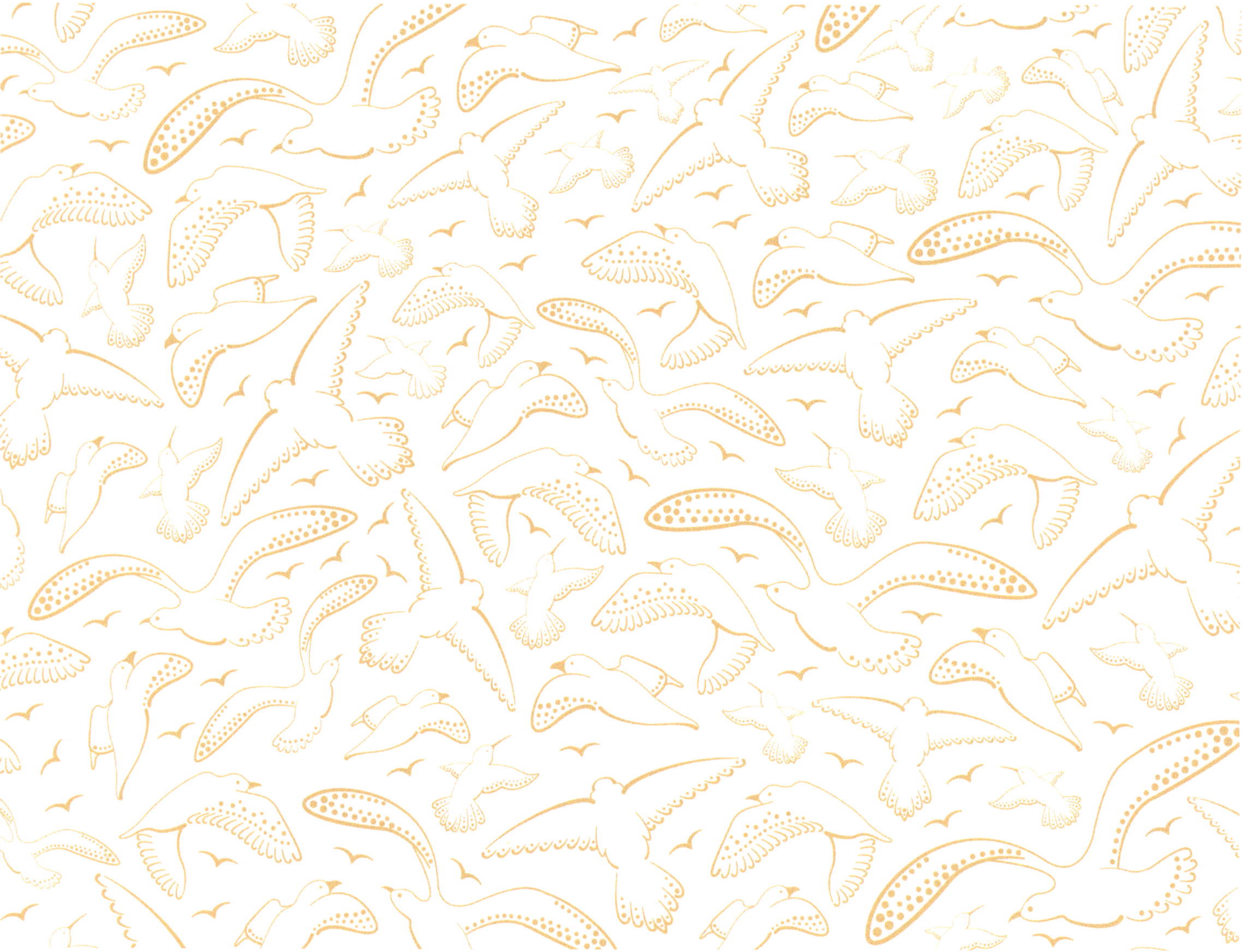

Flying Birds
Mariel Katafias

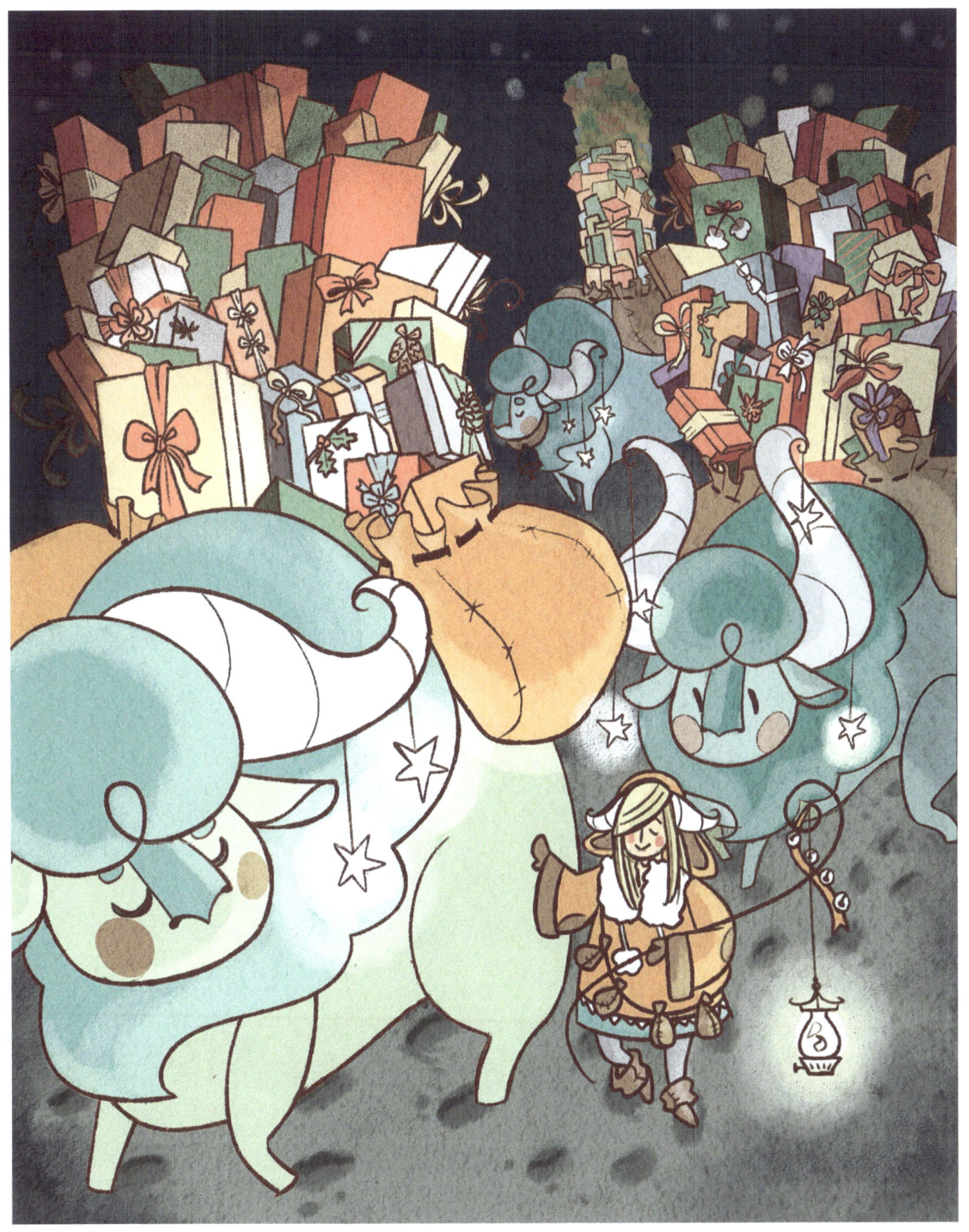

TIM BOWERS JUDGE'S PICK

Star Bison
Kristin Ridgley

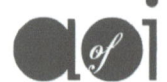

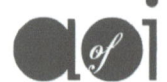

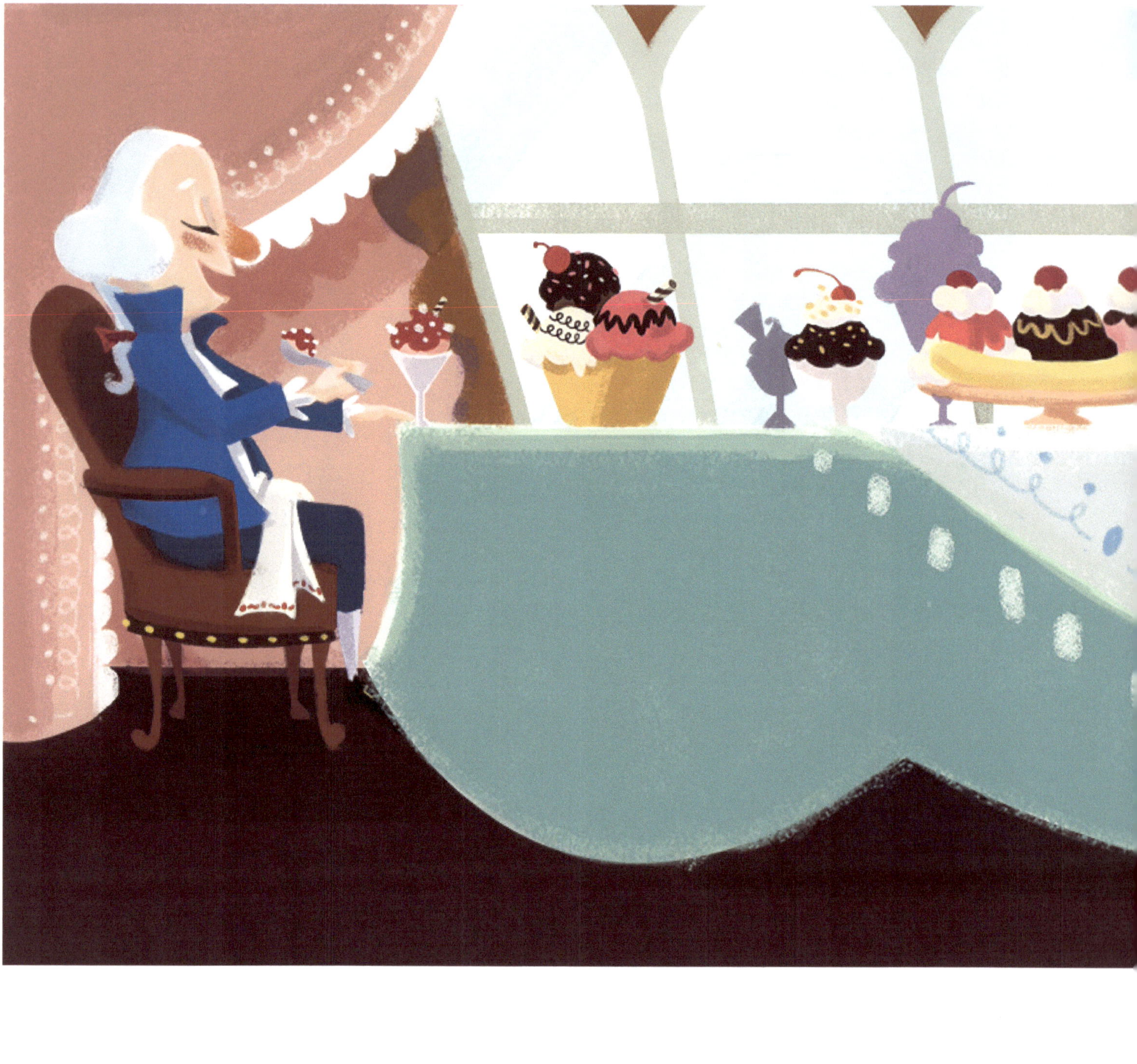

George Washington
Emily Paik

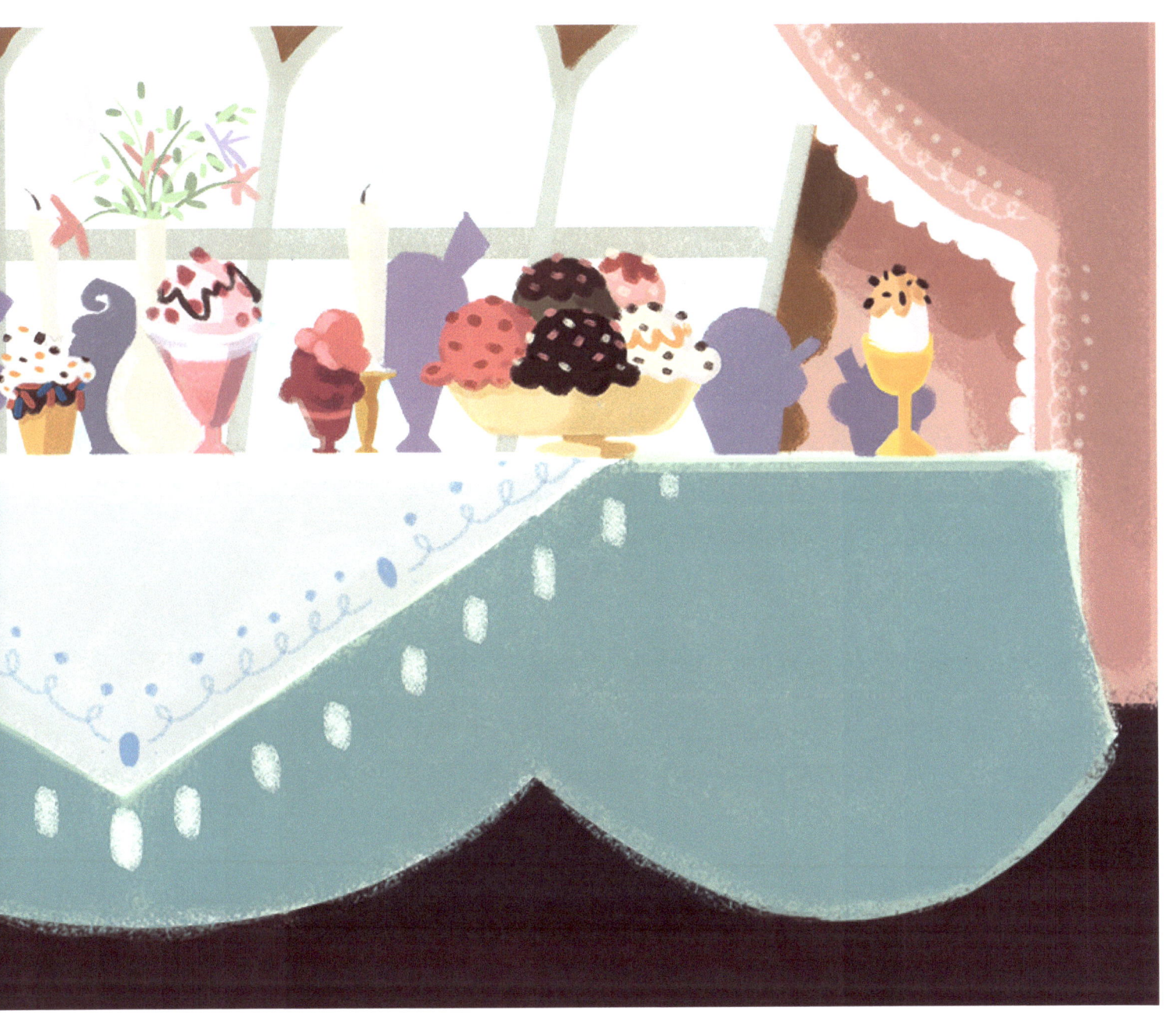

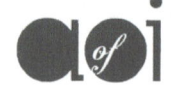

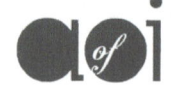

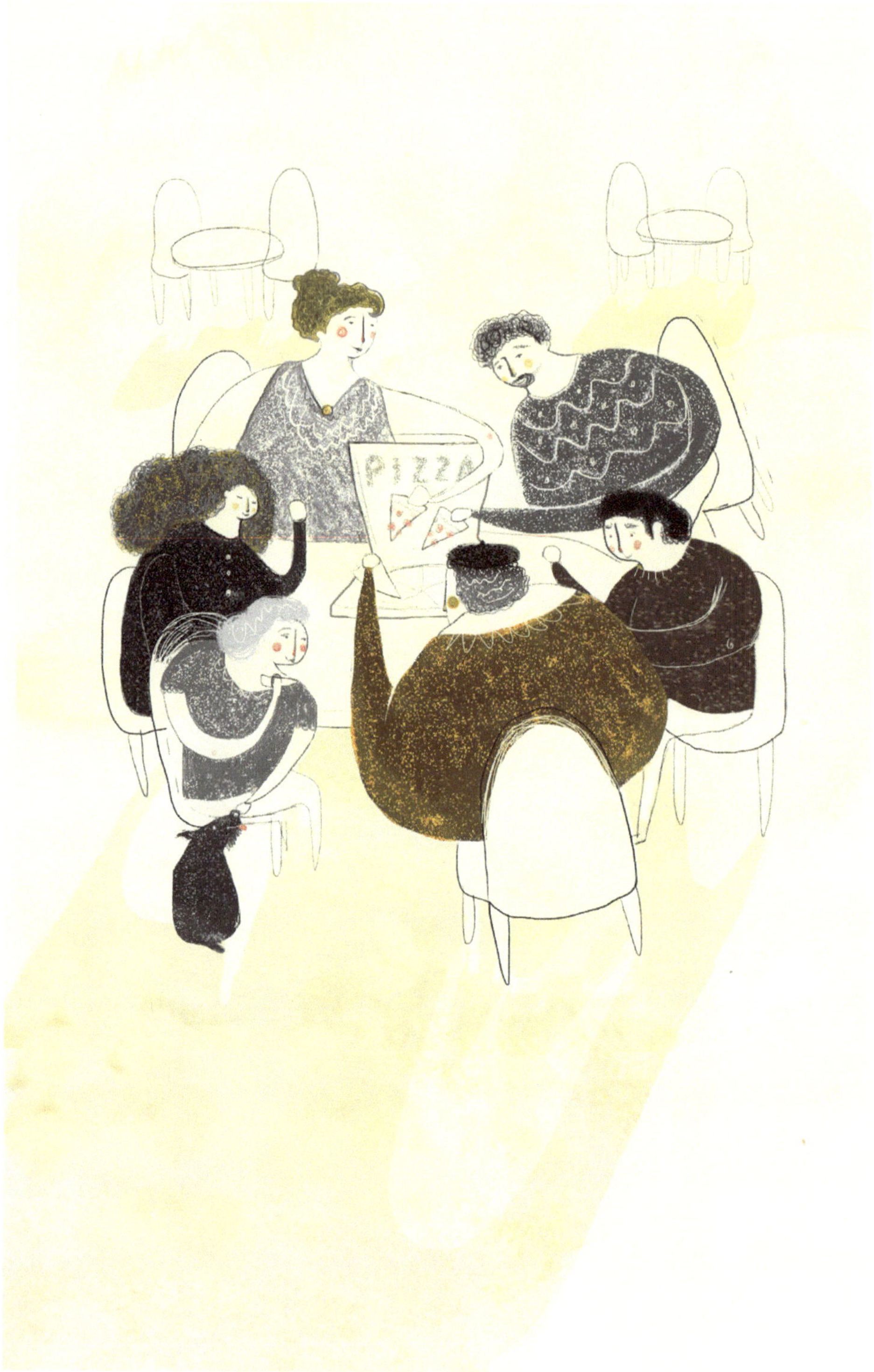

Pizza Eaters
Hannah Ross

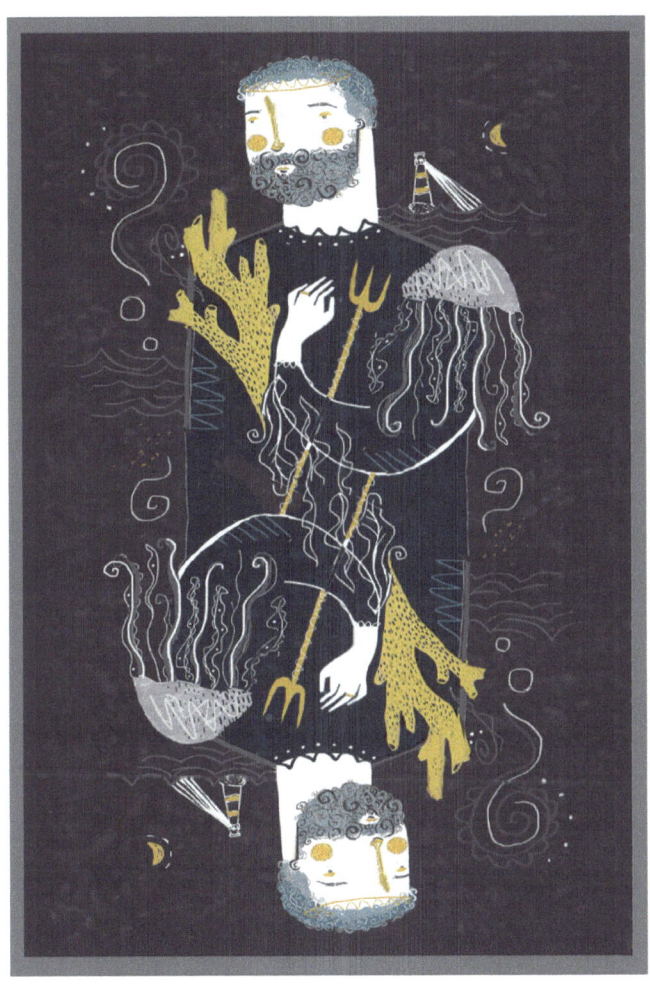
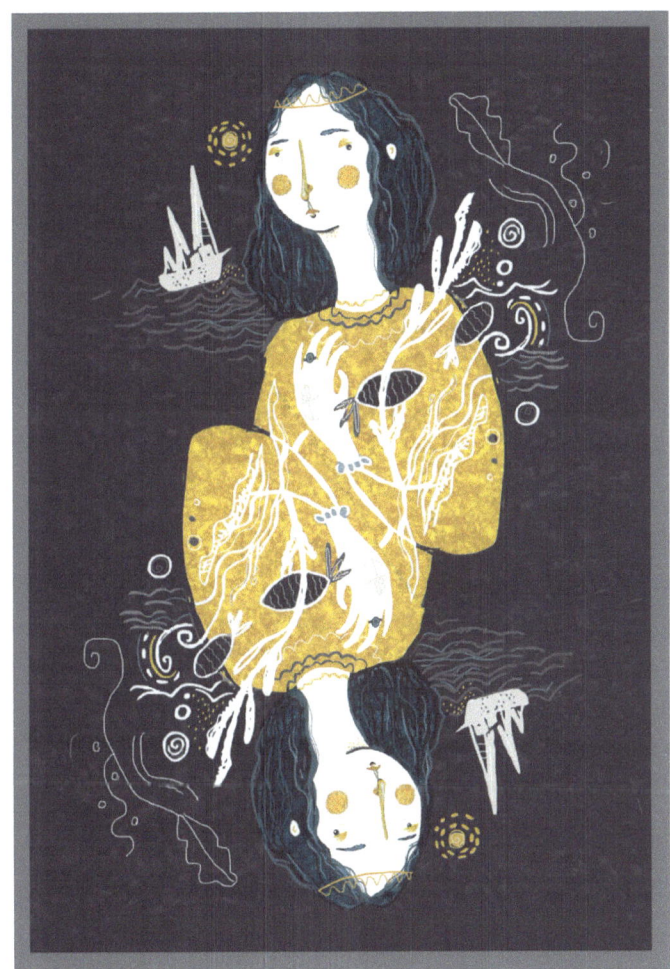

Sea King and Queen
Hannah Ross

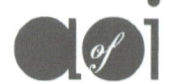

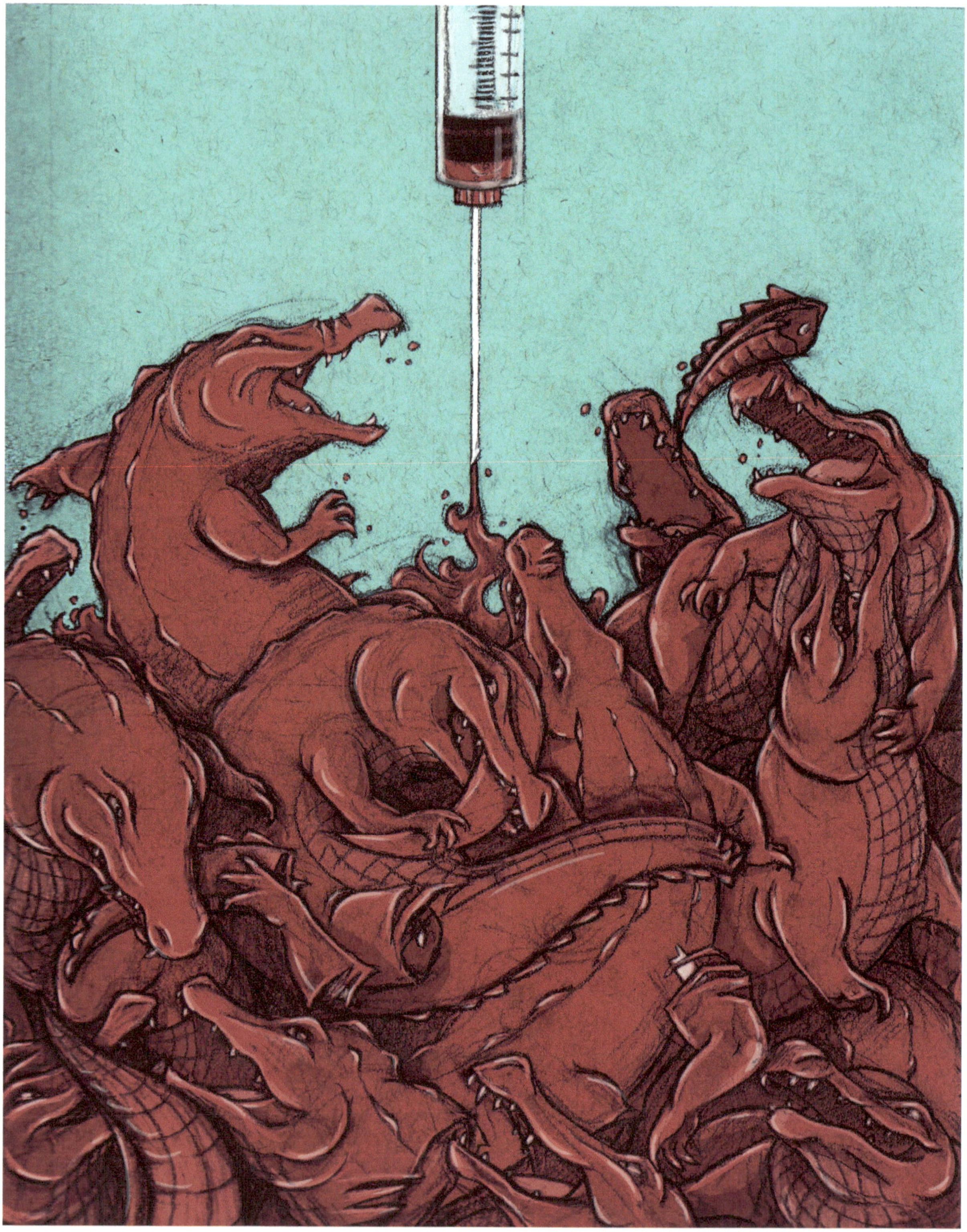

Krokodil
Zayra Feliciano

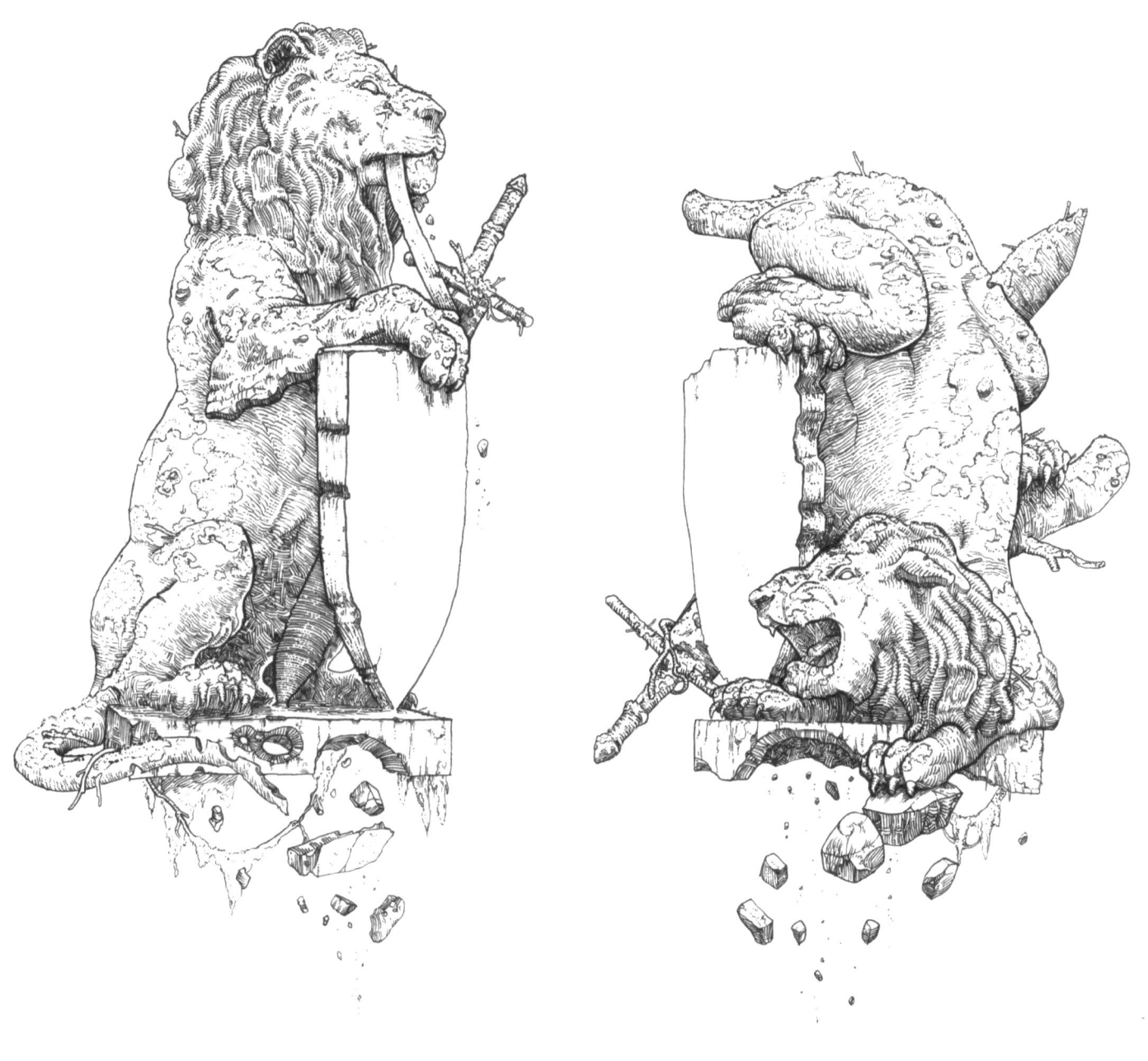

Twin Lions
Samuel Veirs

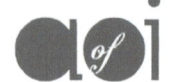

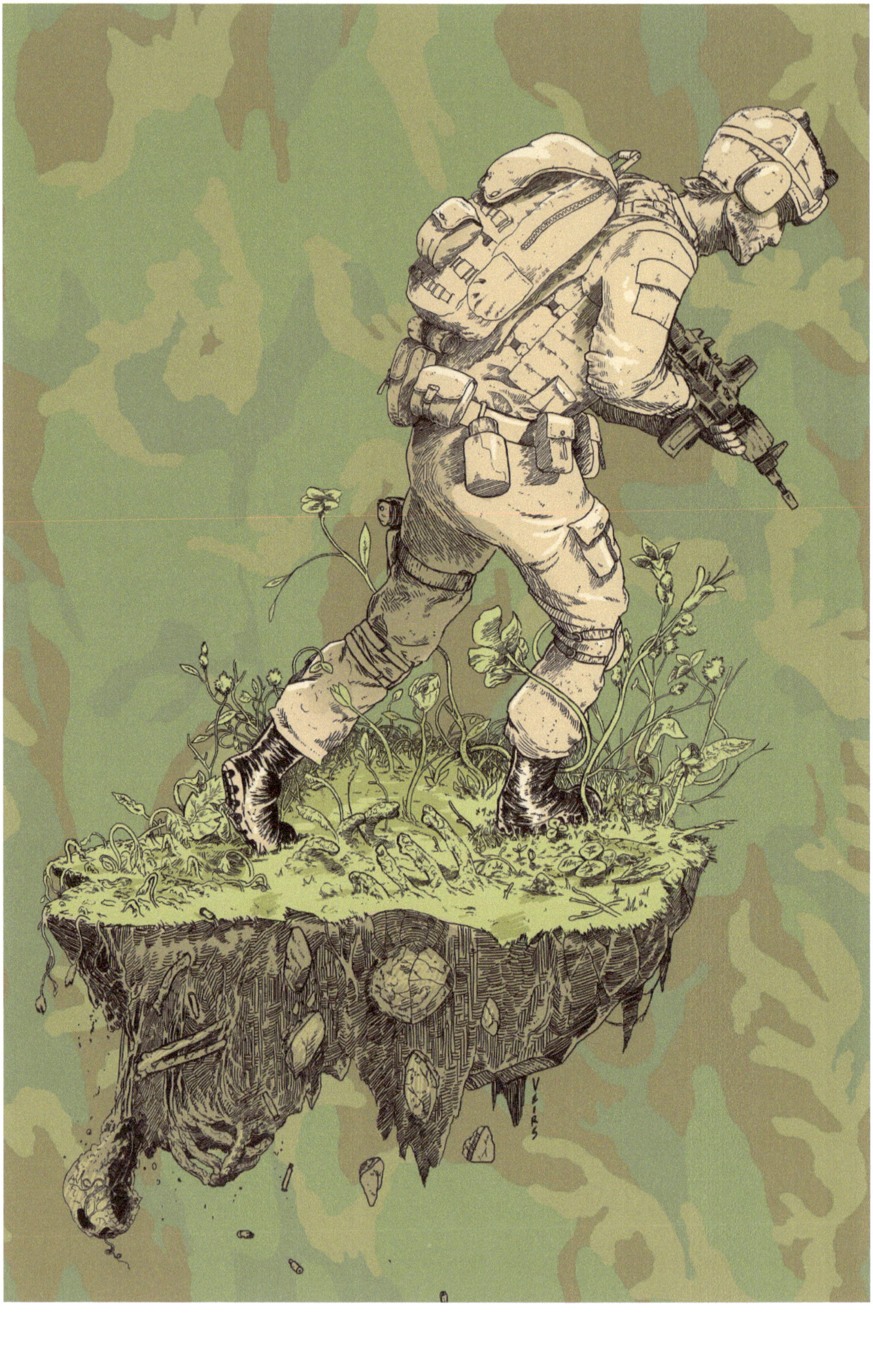

The Soldier
Samuel Veirs

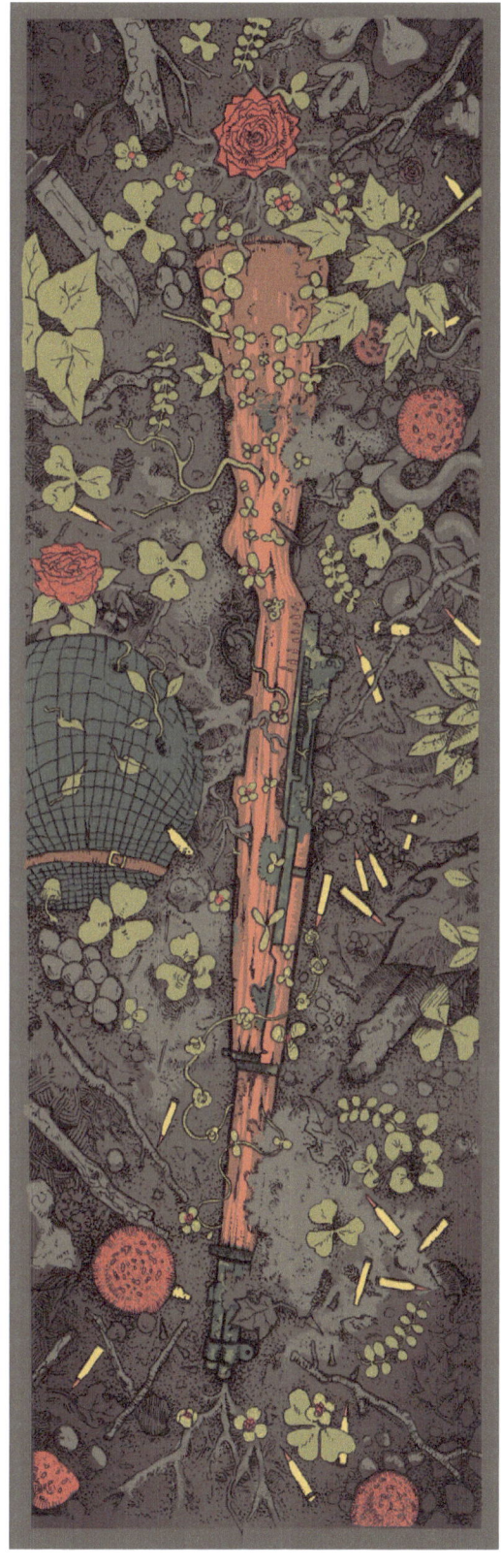

KRISTEN HARRIS JUDGE'S PICK

Life After
Samuel Veirs

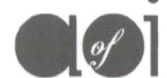

ART OF ILLUSTRATION

2014

April 5th - April 24th

Special Thanks to Laura Kuenzli from
Rivet Gallery

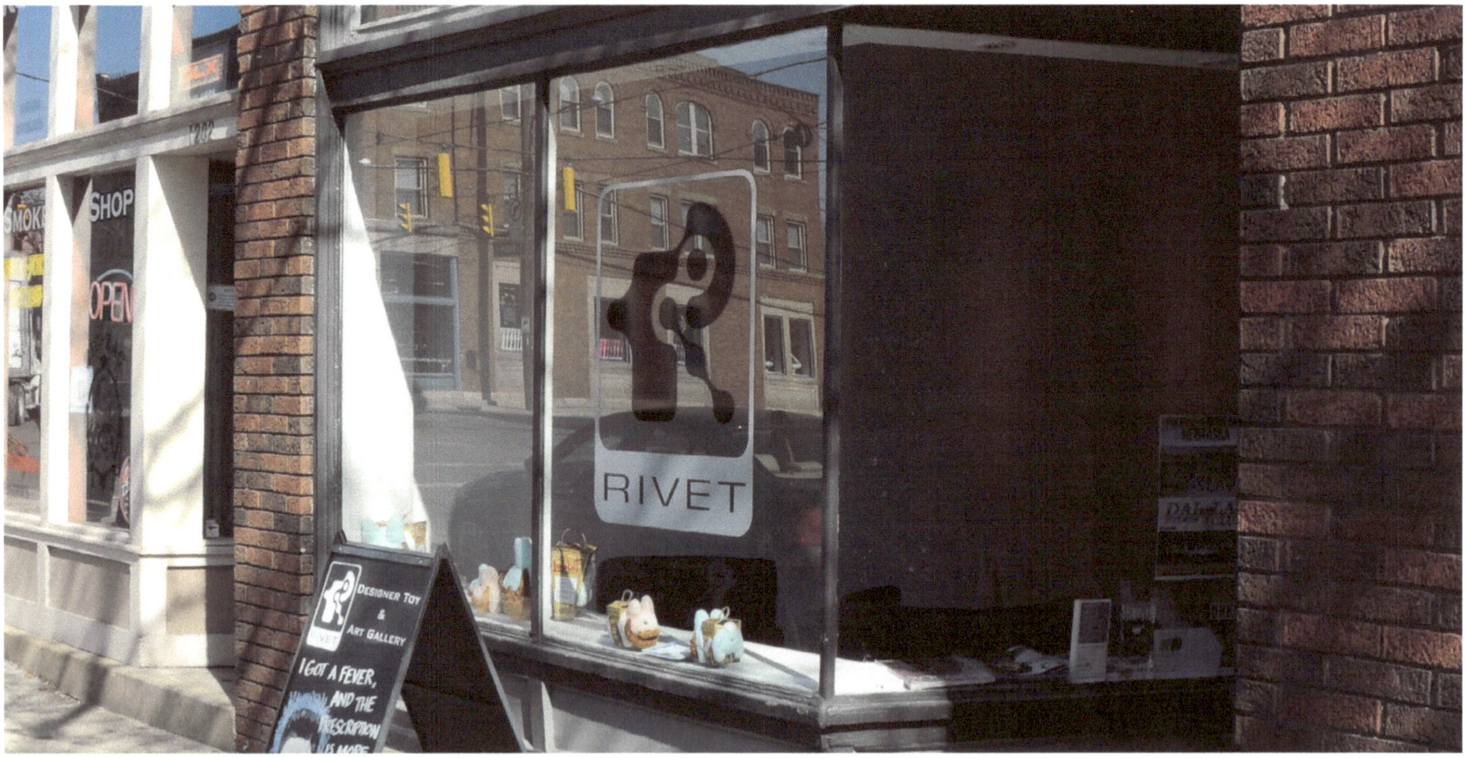

ORGANIZED BY

Samuel Veirs
Hannah Ross
Haleigh Richards
Josh Parkinson
Madeline Miller

EXHIBITION SPONSORS

RIVET GALLERY
39 BELOW FROYO
THE HILLS MARKET
AMC THEATRE

JUDGES

Jeremy Slagle
Kristen Harris
Tim Bowers
Dana Martin Ryan
Krysti Kalkman

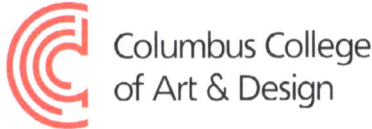

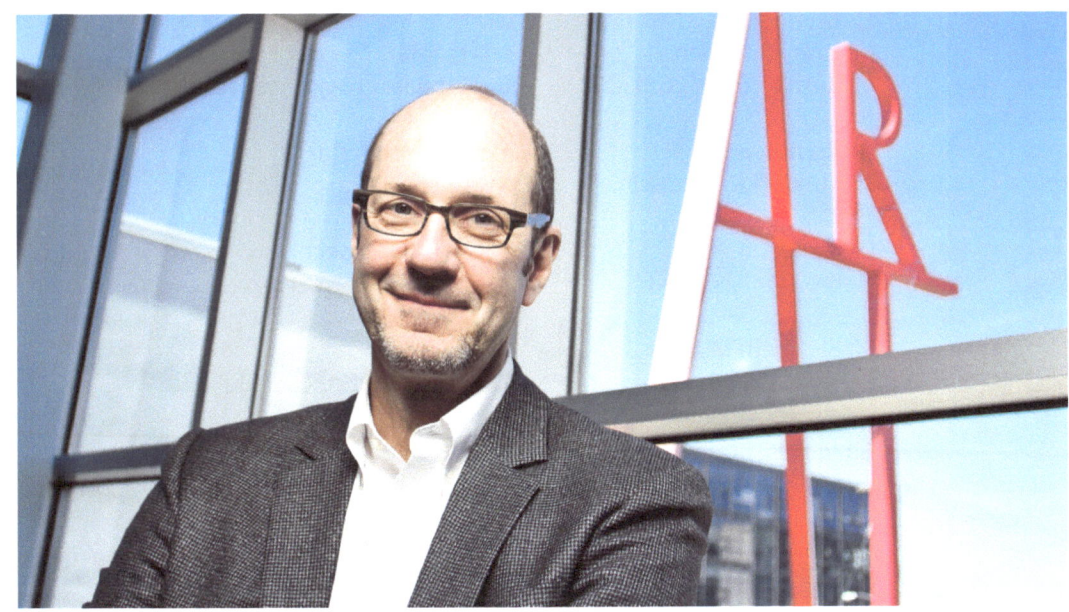

This years AOI show is dedicated to CCAD president Denny Griffith.

Book Design and Layout by Samuel Veirs
Introduction by Hannah Ross
Cover Illustration by Erlson Neba

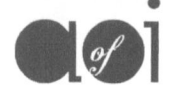

CONTACT INFORMATION

Katherine Fedorco
kfedorco.1@go.ccad.edu

Sarah Buzzard
sarah.e.buzzard@gmail.com

Sophie Lim
slim.1@go.ccad.edu

Katie Vasey
kvasey.1@go.ccad.edu

Kristin Ridgley
kridgley.1@go.ccad.edu

Kristen Starlein
kstarlein.1@go.ccad.edu

Hannah Ross
hross.3@go.ccad.edu

Zayra Feliciano
zfeliciano.1@go.ccad.edu

Josh Parkinson
jparkinson.1@go.ccad.edu

Dorian Lafferre
doriandraws@gmail.com

Emily Paik
SPaik.1@go.ccad.edu

Pornpin Cecchini
Cecchini.Tangmo@gmail.com

Mariel Katafias
mjkatafias@gmail.com

Colleen Clark
cclark.4@go.ccad.edu

Geoffrey Blasiman
gblasiman.1@go.ccad.edu

Emmett Shearer
eshearer.1@go.ccad.edu

Aaron Behnk
abehnk.1@go.ccad.edu

Andrew Peña
apena.1@go.ccad.edu

Cailey Tervo
ctervo.1@go.ccad.edu

Hannah Ploechl
hploechl.1@go.ccad.edu

Kit Elizabeth Mizeres
emizeres.1@go.ccad.edu

Erlson Neba
eneba.1@go.ccad.edu

Anna Vigorito
avigorito.1@go.ccad.edu

Thomas Kirkeberg
tkirkeberg@gmail.com

Emily Graham
egraham.1@go.ccad.edu

Samuel Veirs
samuel.veirs@gmail.com

Alex Kim
92alexkim@gmail.com